ATLASES OF THE WORLD

ATLAS OF
EUROPE

S. JOSHUA COMIRE, MALCOLM PORTER, and KEITH LYE

This edition published in 2010 by:

The Rosen Publishing Group, Inc.
29 East 21st Street
New York, NY 10010

Library of Congress Cataloging-in-Publication Data

Comire, S. Joshua
Atlas of Europe / S. Joshua Comire, Malcolm Porter,
and Keith Lye.
  p. cm. – (Atlases of the world)
Includes index.

ISBN 978-1-4358-8457-1 (library binding)
ISBN 978-1-4358-9114-2 (pbk.)
ISBN 978-1-4358-9120-3 (6-pack)

1. Europe–Maps. I. Porter, Malcolm. II. Lye, Keith.
  III. Rosen Central (Firm) IV. Title.

G1795.C6 2010
912.4–dc22

2009582100

Manufactured in China

This edition published under license from
Cherrytree Books.

JUV
912.4
Com

CPSIA Compliance Information: Batch #EW0102YA: For Further Information
contact Rosen Publishing, New York, New York at 1-800-237-9932

ATLASES OF THE WORLD
ATLAS OF EUROPE

This illustrated atlas combines maps, pictures, flags, globes, information panels, diagrams and charts to give an overview of the whole continent, a closer look at each of its countries and at the Atlantic and Arctic oceans.

COUNTRY CLOSE-UPS

Each double-page spread has these features:

Introduction The author introduces the most important facts about the country or region.

Globes A globe on which you can see the country's or region's position in the continent and the world.

Flags Every country's flag is shown.

Information panels Every country has an information panel that gives its area, population and capital, and where possible its currency, religions, languages, main towns and government.

Pictures Important features of each country are illustrated and captioned to give a flavor of the country. You can find out about physical features, famous people, ordinary people, animals, plants, places, products, and much more.

Maps Every country is shown on a clear, accurate map. To get the most from the maps it helps to know the symbols that are shown in the key on the opposite page.

Land You can see by the coloring on the map where the land is forested, frozen or desert.

Height Relief hill shading shows where the mountain ranges are. Individual mountains are marked by a triangle.

Direction Except for the map of the Arctic, all of the maps are drawn with north at the top of the page.

Scale All of the maps are drawn to scale so that you can find the distance between places in miles or kilometers.

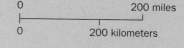

KEY TO MAPS

FRANCE	Country name
Lapland	Region
	Country border
■	More than 1 million people*
●	More than 500,000 people
•	Less than 500,000 people
□	Country capital
ᴬᴸᴾˢ	Mountain range
Mont Blanc ▲ *15,771ft (4,807m)*	Mountain with its height
∴ *Stonehenge*	Archaeological site

Rhine	River
	Canal
	Lake
	Dam
	Island

	Forest
	Crops
	Dry grassland
	Desert
	Tundra
	Polar

Population figures in all cases are estimates, based on the most recent censuses where available or a variety of other sources.

CONTINENT CLOSE-UPS

People and Beliefs Map of population densities; chart of percentage of population by country; chart of areas of countries; map of religions.

Climate and Vegetation Map of vegetation from polar to desert; maps of winter and summer temperatures; map of annual rainfall.

Ecology and Environment Map of environmental damage to land and sea; maps showing deaths caused by heart disease, cancers and fatal road accidents; panel on endangered animals and plants.

Economy Map of agricultural and industrial products; chart of gross domestic product for individual countries; panel on per capita gross domestic products; map of sources of energy.

Politics and History Panel of great events; map of location of major events in European history; timeline of important dates; maps of prehistoric sites, the Roman Empire, 20th century conflicts and the European Community.

Oceans Maps of the Atlantic and Arctic oceans, and panels of statistics.

CONTENTS

EUROPE 4

COUNTRY CLOSE-UPS

CONTINENT CLOSE-UPS

Reindeer
see page 7

EUROPE

Europe is the sixth largest continent, covering about seven percent of the world's land area. Only Australia is smaller. Europe was the home of several major civilizations and its culture has had a great influence on the rest of the world.

In the east, Europe borders Asia. The boundary with Asia runs along the Ural Mountains and the Ural River to the Caspian Sea and then through the Caucasus Mountains. About a quarter of Russia lies in Europe, while the rest is in Asia. Smaller parts of four other countries also lie in Europe.

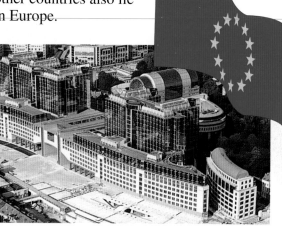

European Union This is an alliance of 27 European countries that work together to create a single economy and, through friendly cooperation, promote democracy and prevent wars. The headquarters is in Brussels (above), the parliament in Strasbourg.

Napoleon I (1769-1821) was a great military leader who became emperor of France. His armies conquered an empire that covered most of central and western Europe. Europe has been the scene of many great wars.

EUROPE
Area: 4,032,000sq miles (10,443,000sq km)
Population: 700,000,000
Number of independent countries: 44
(including European Russia, but not Azerbaijan, Georgia, Kazakhstan and Turkey, which are mainly in Asia)

ICELAND

ATLANTIC OCEAN

NORWAY

SWEDEN

North Sea

IRELAND

UNITED KINGDOM

DENMARK

Baltic Sea

NETHERLANDS

BELGIUM GERMANY POLAND

LUXEMBOURG

CZECH REP.

Bay of Biscay

FRANCE LIECHTENSTEIN SLOVAKIA

SWITZERLAND AUSTRIA

HUNGARY

SLOVENIA

CROATIA

ANDORRA MONACO SAN MARINO BOSNIA & HERZEGOVINA

PORTUGAL ITALY

MONTENEGRO

SPAIN

VATICAN CITY

GIBRALTAR (UK)

MEDITERRANEAN SEA

MALTA

0	250 miles
0	250 kilometers

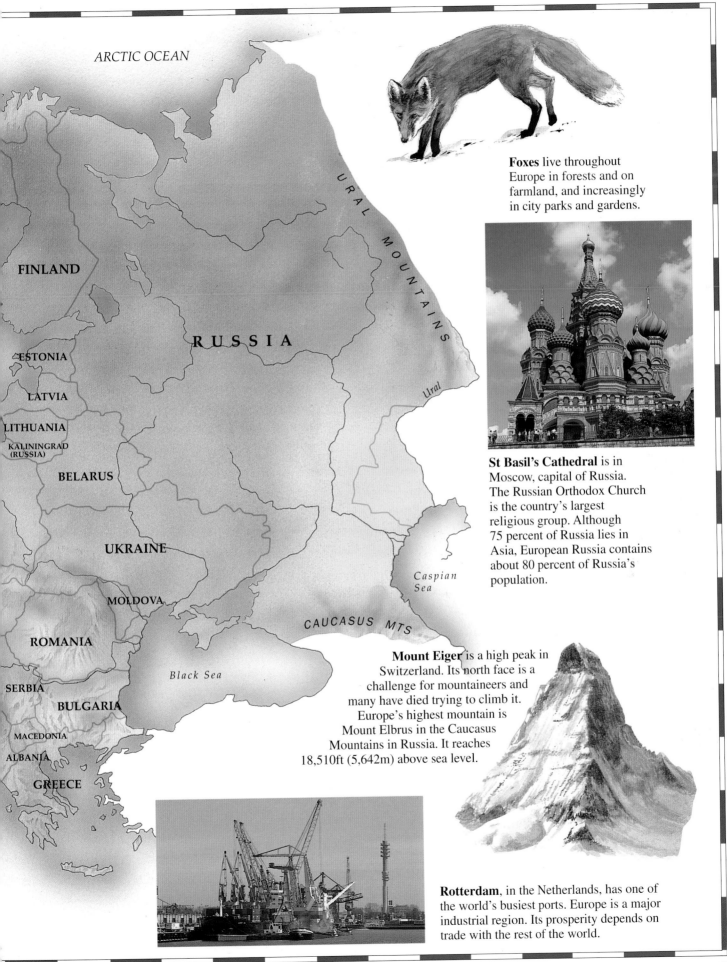

ARCTIC OCEAN

Foxes live throughout Europe in forests and on farmland, and increasingly in city parks and gardens.

FINLAND

ESTONIA

LATVIA

LITHUANIA

KALININGRAD (RUSSIA)

BELARUS

URAL MOUNTAINS

RUSSIA

Ural

St Basil's Cathedral is in Moscow, capital of Russia. The Russian Orthodox Church is the country's largest religious group. Although 75 percent of Russia lies in Asia, European Russia contains about 80 percent of Russia's population.

UKRAINE

MOLDOVA

Caspian Sea

CAUCASUS MTS

ROMANIA

Black Sea

SERBIA

BULGARIA

MACEDONIA

ALBANIA

GREECE

Mount Eiger is a high peak in Switzerland. Its north face is a challenge for mountaineers and many have died trying to climb it. Europe's highest mountain is Mount Elbrus in the Caucasus Mountains in Russia. It reaches 18,510ft (5,642m) above sea level.

Rotterdam, in the Netherlands, has one of the world's busiest ports. Europe is a major industrial region. Its prosperity depends on trade with the rest of the world.

NORTHERN EUROPE

Northern Europe contains Scandinavia, a region that consists of Norway and Sweden. It also includes Finland and the small country of Denmark.

   The climate is mostly unsuitable for farming, except in the south. The region's resources include Norway's oil, which it gets from the North Sea, its many rivers, which are used to produce hydroelectricity, and huge forests. Manufacturing is now the most valuable activity in all four countries.

DENMARK

Area: 16,639sq miles (43,094sq km)
Highest point: 568ft (173m)
Population: 5,451,000
Capital and largest city: Copenhagen (pop 1,066,000)
Other large cities: Århus (229,000) Odense (146,000) Ålborg (122,000)
Official language: Danish
Religion: Christianity (Lutheran 95%)
Government: Monarchy
Currency: Danish krone

FINLAND

Area: 130,559sq miles (338,145sq km)
Highest point: Mount Haltia 4,344ft (1,324m)
Population: 5,231,000
Capital and largest city: Helsinki (pop 1,075,000)
Other large cities: Espoo (224,000), Tampere (201,000), Vantaa (184,000), Turku (175,000), Oulu (126,000)
Official languages: Finnish, Swedish
Religion: Christianity (Lutheran 84%)
Government: Republic
Currency: Euro

NORWAY

Area: 125,050sq miles (323,877sq km)
Highest point: Galdhøppigen 8,100ft (2,469m)
Population: 4,612,000
Capital and largest city: Oslo (pop 795,000)
Other large cities: Bergen (211,000) Stavanger (169,000) Trondheim (144,000)
Official language: Norwegian
Religion: Christianity (Lutheran 85%)
Government: Monarchy
Currency: Norwegian krone

Fiords are long, narrow inlets of sea that stretch along the ragged, mountainous coast of Norway. One of them, called Sogne Fiord, extends 124 miles (200km) inland.

Oil is extracted from deposits under the North Sea. Fuels and fuel products are Norway's leading exports. Farming, forestry, fishing and manufacturing are other major activities in northern Europe.

SWEDEN

Area: 173,732sq miles (449,964sq km)
Highest point: Mount Kebnekaise 6,926ft (2,111m)
Population: 9,017,000
Capital and largest city: Stockholm (pop 1,697,000)
Other large cities: Göteborg (481,000) Malmö (269,000)
Official language: Swedish
Religion: Christianity (Church of Sweden 87%)
Government: Monarchy
Currency: Swedish krona

ATLANTIC OCEAN

Trondheim

Ålesund

Galdhøppigen 8,100ft (2,469m)

Bergen

NORWAY

Glåma

Oslo

Stavanger

Skien

Fredrikstad

Kristiansand

Lake Vänern

Skagerrak

Lake Vättern

Borås

North Sea

Ålborg

Göteborg

Kattegat

Jutland

Växjö

Århus

568ft (173m)

DENMARK

Esbjerg

Copenhagen

Odense

Malmö

Bornholm

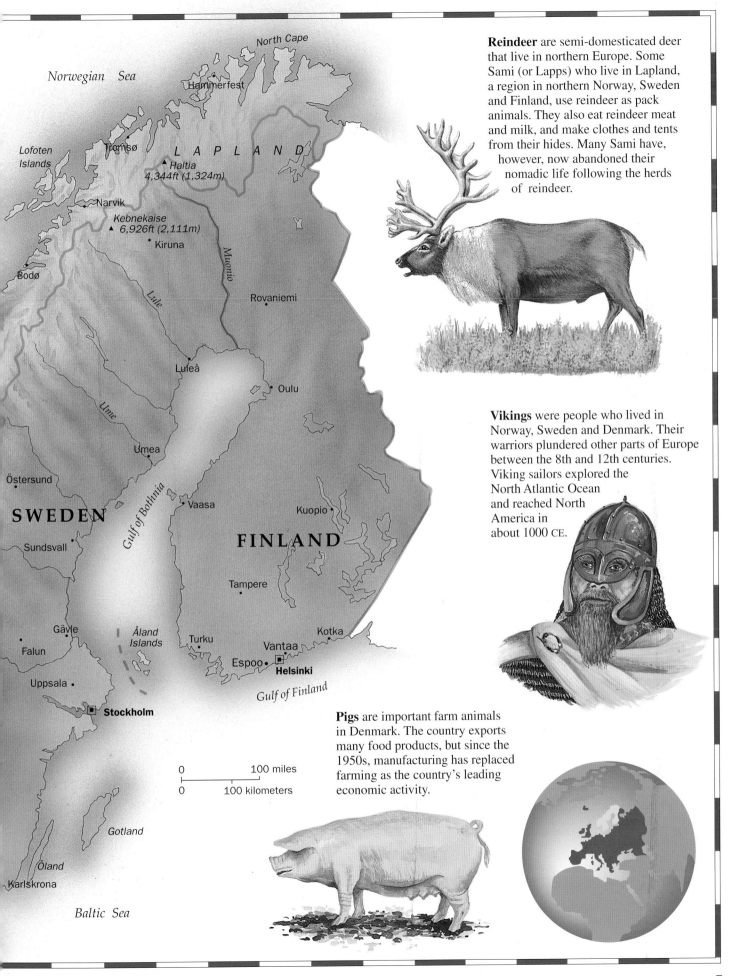

Reindeer are semi-domesticated deer that live in northern Europe. Some Sami (or Lapps) who live in Lapland, a region in northern Norway, Sweden and Finland, use reindeer as pack animals. They also eat reindeer meat and milk, and make clothes and tents from their hides. Many Sami have, however, now abandoned their nomadic life following the herds of reindeer.

Vikings were people who lived in Norway, Sweden and Denmark. Their warriors plundered other parts of Europe between the 8th and 12th centuries. Viking sailors explored the North Atlantic Ocean and reached North America in about 1000 CE.

Pigs are important farm animals in Denmark. The country exports many food products, but since the 1950s, manufacturing has replaced farming as the country's leading economic activity.

Norwegian Sea

North Cape

Hammerfest

Lofoten Islands

Tromsø

L A P L A N D

▲ Haltia
4,344ft (1,324m)

Narvik

Kebnekaise
▲ 6,926ft (2,111m)

Kiruna

Bodø

Muonio

Lule

Rovaniemi

Luleå

Ume

Oulu

Umea

Östersund

Gulf of Bothnia

Vaasa

Kuopio

SWEDEN

FINLAND

Sundsvall

Tampere

Gävle

Åland Islands

Turku

Kotka

Falun

Vantaa

Espoo

Helsinki

Uppsala

Gulf of Finland

■ **Stockholm**

0   100 miles

0   100 kilometers

Gotland

Öland

Karlskrona

Baltic Sea

ICELAND

Iceland, in the North Atlantic Ocean, is often called the "land of ice and fire." Large bodies of ice cover about one-eighth of the land and the country has about 200 volcanoes. The main industry is fishing and fish processing.

 ICELAND

Area: 39,769sq miles (103,000sq km)
Highest point: Hvannadalshnúkur 6,952ft (2,119m)
Population: 299,000
Capital: Reykjavik (pop 184,000)
Official language: Icelandic
Religion: Christianity (Lutheran 85%)
Government: Republic
Currency: Icelandic krona

Geysers are hot springs that throw up high jets of steam and hot water. The water is heated by underground volcanic rocks. It is used to heat buildings and supply homes with hot tap water.

Fishing is important in the waters around Iceland. Fish and fish products account for more than half of the country's exports. Iceland has little farmland, though some farmers keep sheep and cattle.

Isafjördhur

Siglufjördhur

Blönduos Akureyri

Seydisfjördhur

I C E L A N D

Hofn

Vatnajökull

Keflavik □ Reykjavik
Hafnarfjördhur

▲ Hvannadalshnúkur
6,952ft (2,119m)

ATLANTIC OCEAN

Heimaey

Vik

Surtsey

| 0 | | 50 miles |
| 0 | | 50 kilometers |

Surtsey is a volcanic island that appeared off southern Iceland in 1963. It was named after Surt, the Norse god of fire.

IRELAND

Ireland consists of the Republic of Ireland, which makes up five-sixths of the island, and Northern Ireland, which is part of the United Kingdom (see page 10). Farming is important in Ireland, but manufacturing and new technology and service industries are the most valuable activities.

IRELAND

Area: 27,137sq miles (70,284sq km)
Highest point: Carrauntoohill 3,415ft (1,041m)
Population: 4,062,000
Capital and largest city: Dublin (pop 1,015,000)
Other large cities: Cork (186,000)
Official languages: Irish, English
Religion: Christianity (Roman Catholic 88%)
Government: Republic
Currency: Euro

Giant's Causeway is probably Northern Ireland's best-known tourist attraction. It was formed when molten lava cooled to form masses of six-sided columns made of a rock called basalt.

Shamrock is Ireland's national symbol. It is a kind of clover that, according to legend, St Patrick planted. Its three leaves represent the Holy Trinity.

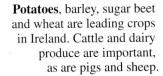

Potatoes, barley, sugar beet and wheat are leading crops in Ireland. Cattle and dairy produce are important, as are pigs and sheep.

Celtic crosses and other carved stone monuments are found throughout Ireland.

UNITED KINGDOM

The United Kingdom of Great Britain and Northern Ireland (often called the UK, or Britain) includes England, Scotland and Wales, which are together called Great Britain, and Northern Ireland (see map on page 9).

The Industrial Revolution began in England in the late 18th century and today the country plays a major part in world trade. It contains some of the most densely populated areas in Europe.

UNITED KINGDOM

Area: 93,941sq miles (243,305sq km)
Highest point: Ben Nevis 4,406ft (1,343m)
Population: 60,609,000
Capital and largest city: London (pop 7,619,000)
Other large cities: Birmingham (2,243,000)
Manchester (2,223,000)
Leeds (1,417,000)
Official language: English
Religion: Christianity (71%)
Government: Monarchy
Currency: Pound sterling

ENGLAND
Area: 50,346sq miles (130,395sq km)
Population: 50,911,000
Capital: London (pop 7,619,000)

NORTHERN IRELAND
Area: 5,345sq miles (13,843sq km)
Population: 1,703,000
Capital: Belfast (pop 277,000)

SCOTLAND
Area: 30,237sq miles (78,313sq km)
Population: 5,057,000
Capital: Edinburgh (pop 449,000)

WALES
Area: 8,013sq miles (20,754sq km)
Population: 2,938,000
Capital: Cardiff (pop 305,000)

ISLE OF MAN & CHANNEL ISLANDS
The Isle of Man in the Irish Sea and the Channel Islands off the coast of northwest France are British dependencies, but they are not part of the United Kingdom.

William Shakespeare (1564-1616) is widely regarded as the world's greatest poet and dramatist. Britain has also produced many other celebrated writers, and the language in which they have written is now spoken in many countries.

Stonehenge is an ancient monument in southern England. It is a circle of huge stones that were probably used for religious purposes. It was built between about 2800 and 1500 BCE.

Sheep are raised in highland areas, cattle and pigs on lowland farms. Agriculture is important but the country imports food. Most of its wealth comes from manufacturing, trade and services such as banking, insurance, finance and tourism.

John o' Groats
Wick
Lewis
Hebrides
North West Highlands
Skye
Inverness
Loch Ness
Spey
Grampian Mts
Fort William
Ben Nevis 4,406ft (1,343m)
Dundee
Perth
Loch Lomond
SCOTLAND
Glasgow Clyde **Edinburgh**
Ayr
Dumfries
Carlisle
Isle of Man
Scafell Pike 3,209ft (978
Douglas
Blackpool
Liverpool
Bangor
Snowdon 3,560ft (1,085m)
IRISH SEA
WALES
Aberystwyth
Swansea
Newport
Cardiff
Bristol
Exeter
Plymouth
Penzance
Land's End
Isles of Scilly

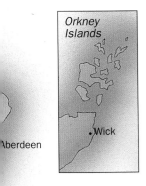

Orkney
Islands

Wick

Shetland
Islands

Lerwick

Aberdeen

Golf developed in Scotland, where the first organized golf club was set up in 1744. Soccer is, however, by far the most popular sport in the United Kingdom.

NORTH SEA

Berwick-upon-Tweed

Newcastle upon Tyne
Sunderland
Middlesbrough

London Eye Built by the River Thames to mark the millennium, this observation wheel is 443ft (135m) high. From the top you can see for 25 miles (40km).

Puffins are sea birds found mostly on the north and west coasts of Britain. The country has many animal species, though numbers have declined because of human population pressures and pollution.

York
Bradford
Leeds
Kingston upon Hull
Manchester
Sheffield
toke-on-Trent
Derby
Nottingham

ENGLAND
Leicester
Norwich
Wolverhampton
Coventry
Birmingham
Cambridge
Northampton
Ipswich

Oxford
Luton
Thames
Reading
London

Stonehenge
Dover
Southampton
Brighton
Portsmouth
Bournemouth
Isle of Wight

English Channel

Channel Islands

Guernsey

FRANCE

Jersey

London was founded by the Romans in 43 CE on the River Thames. It has many historic buildings. The business heart of London, called the City of London, is an internationally important financial center.

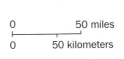

0   50 miles
0   50 kilometers

LOW COUNTRIES

The Low Countries lie at the western end of a huge plain that extends across Europe from the North Sea to the Ural Mountains in Russia. Much of the land is flat. Large areas, especially in the Netherlands, were once under the sea. They would still be flooded if the Dutch had not built dikes (strong sea walls). Farming is important in this region, but manufacturing is the most valuable activity.

BELGIUM

Area: 11,783sq miles (30,519sq km)
Highest point: Botrange Mountain 2,277ft (694m)
Population: 10,379,000
Capital and largest city: Brussels (pop 1,000,000)
Other large cities: Antwerp (455,000) Ghent (229,000)
Official languages: Dutch, French, German
Religion: Christianity (Roman Catholic 75%)
Government: Federal monarchy
Currency: Euro

LUXEMBOURG

Area: 998sq miles (2,586sq km)
Highest point: Buurgplatz 1,834ft (559m)
Population: 474,000
Capital: Luxembourg (pop 77,000)
Languages: Luxemburgian, French, German
Religion: Christianity (Roman Catholic 87%)
Government: Monarchy (Grand Duchy)
Currency: Euro

NETHERLANDS

Area: 15,770sq miles (40,844sq km)
Highest point: 1,053ft (321m)
Population: 16,491,000
Capital and largest city: Amsterdam (pop 736,000)
Other large cities: Rotterdam (599,000) The Hague (458,000)
Official language: Dutch
Religion: Christianity (Roman Catholic 31%, Dutch Reform Church 13%, Calvinist 7%)
Government: Monarchy
Currency: Euro

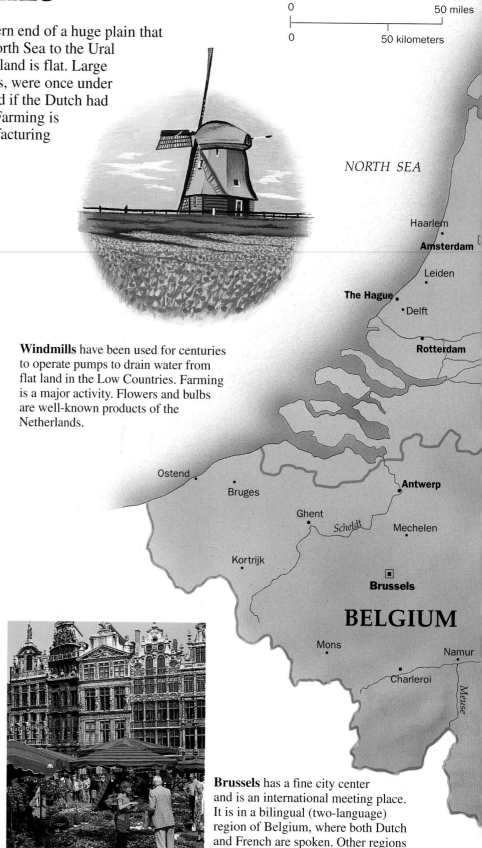

Windmills have been used for centuries to operate pumps to drain water from flat land in the Low Countries. Farming is a major activity. Flowers and bulbs are well-known products of the Netherlands.

Brussels has a fine city center and is an international meeting place. It is in a bilingual (two-language) region of Belgium, where both Dutch and French are spoken. Other regions include the Dutch-speaking Flemish Region in the north and the French-speaking Walloon Region in the south.

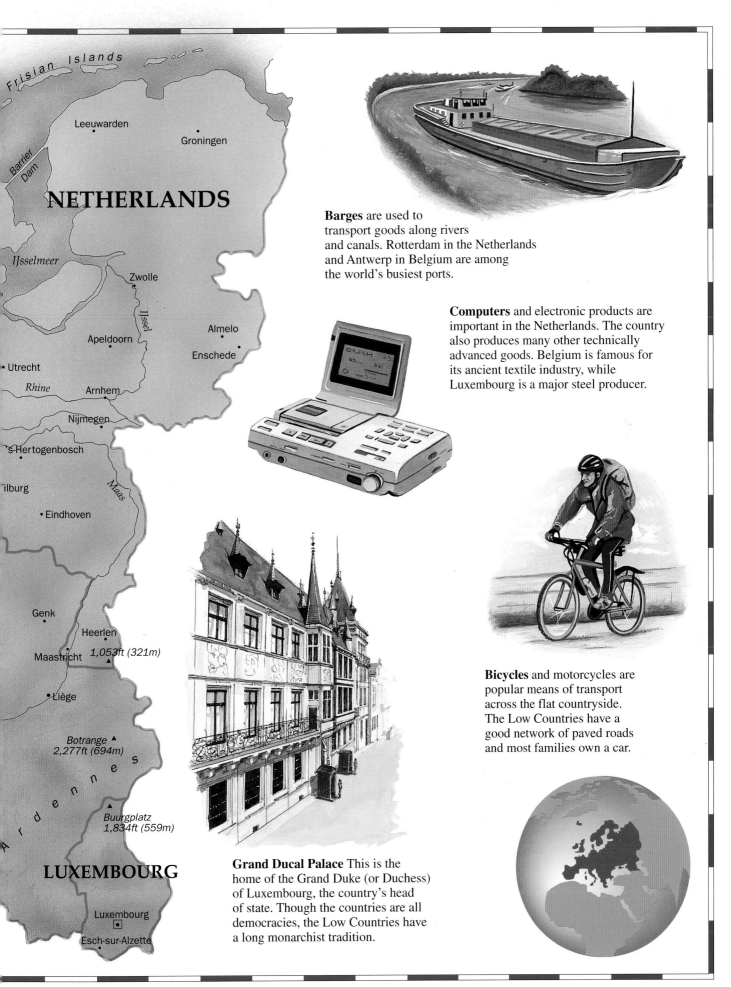

NETHERLANDS

Frisian Islands

Leeuwarden

Groningen

Barrier Dam

IJsselmeer

Zwolle

IJssel

Apeldoorn

Almelo

Enschede

Utrecht

Rhine

Arnhem

Nijmegen

's-Hertogenbosch

Tilburg

Maas

Eindhoven

Genk

Heerlen

1,053ft (321m)

Maastricht

Liège

Botrange ▲
2,277ft (694m)

Ardennes

Buurgplatz
1,834ft (559m)

LUXEMBOURG

Luxembourg

Esch-sur-Alzette

Barges are used to transport goods along rivers and canals. Rotterdam in the Netherlands and Antwerp in Belgium are among the world's busiest ports.

Computers and electronic products are important in the Netherlands. The country also produces many other technically advanced goods. Belgium is famous for its ancient textile industry, while Luxembourg is a major steel producer.

Bicycles and motorcycles are popular means of transport across the flat countryside. The Low Countries have a good network of paved roads and most families own a car.

Grand Ducal Palace This is the home of the Grand Duke (or Duchess) of Luxembourg, the country's head of state. Though the countries are all democracies, the Low Countries have a long monarchist tradition.

GERMANY

In 1945, at the end of World War II, Germany was in ruins. From 1949, it was divided into two parts. West Germany, with aid from western countries including the United States, recovered quickly from the war. It soon became a prosperous industrial democracy. East Germany, under a Communist government, was much less prosperous. The two Germanies were reunited in 1990. This was the first of several major changes to the map of Europe that occurred during the 1990s.

GERMANY

Area: 137,831sq miles (356,980sq km)
Highest point: Zugspitze, near the Austrian border, 9,721ft (2,963m)
Population: 82,422,000
Capital and largest city: Berlin (pop 3,388,000)
Other large cities: Hamburg (1,743,000)
Munich (1,248,000)
Cologne (966,000)
Frankfurt-am-Main (644,000)
Essen (590,000)
Official language: German
Religions: Christianity (Lutheran 34%, Roman Catholic 34%), Islam 4%
Government: Federal republic
Currency: Euro

Storks can often be seen perching on nests on chimney pots. Birds and other wildlife in Germany have suffered from pollution, including acid rain, which has damaged the country's forests.

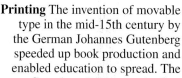

Printing The invention of movable type in the mid-15th century by the German Johannes Gutenberg speeded up book production and enabled education to spread. The Gutenberg Bible was the first Bible produced by movable type.

Brandenburg Gate This monument, built in 1791, became a symbol of a divided Europe. It stood close to the wall that the Communist East German government built to prevent unauthorized crossings to the West. When the wall came down in 1989, Germans gathered at the gate to celebrate.

NORTH SEA

Flensburg
Bremerhaven
Hamburg
Oldenburg
Bremen
Hanover
Osnabrück
Münster
Bielefeld
Weser
Dortmund
Duisburg
Essen
Düsseldorf
Wuppertal
Mönchengladbach
Kassel
Cologne
Aachen
Bonn
Rhine
Koblenz
Eifel
Frankfurt-am-Main
Wiesbaden
Mosel
Mainz
Darmstadt
Mannheim
Saarbrücken
Karlsruhe
Baden-Baden
Stuttgart
Ulm
Black Forest
Freiburg
Ravensburg
Lake Constance

G E R M

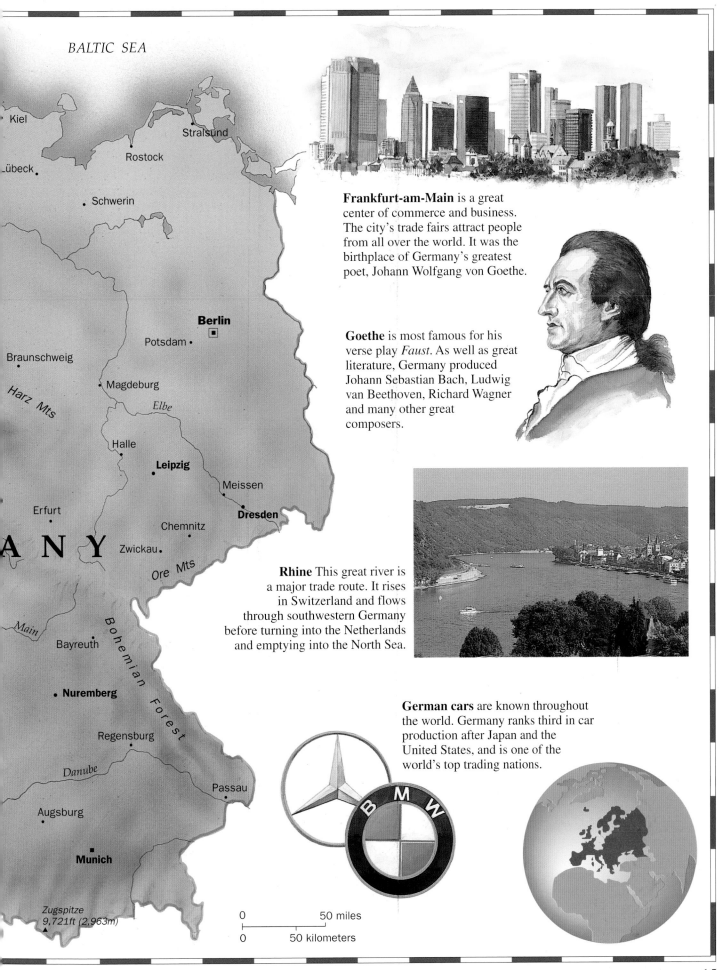

BALTIC SEA

Kiel

Stralsund

Rostock

Lübeck

Schwerin

Braunschweig

Harz Mts

Berlin

Potsdam

Magdeburg

Elbe

Halle

Leipzig

Meissen

Erfurt

Dresden

Chemnitz

Zwickau

ANY

Ore Mts

Main

Bayreuth

Bohemian Forest

Nuremberg

Regensburg

Danube

Passau

Augsburg

Munich

Zugspitze
9,721ft (2,963m)

0   50 miles

0   50 kilometers

Frankfurt-am-Main is a great center of commerce and business. The city's trade fairs attract people from all over the world. It was the birthplace of Germany's greatest poet, Johann Wolfgang von Goethe.

Goethe is most famous for his verse play *Faust*. As well as great literature, Germany produced Johann Sebastian Bach, Ludwig van Beethoven, Richard Wagner and many other great composers.

Rhine This great river is a major trade route. It rises in Switzerland and flows through southwestern Germany before turning into the Netherlands and emptying into the North Sea.

German cars are known throughout the world. Germany ranks third in car production after Japan and the United States, and is one of the world's top trading nations.

MIDDLE EUROPE

Middle Europe consists of Switzerland, Austria and the tiny principality of Liechtenstein, which is sandwiched between them. Western Europe's highest mountain range, the Alps, runs through the region. The magnificent scenery and winter sports draw many tourists to the area. Manufacturing is important and the countries are prosperous. Switzerland is famous for its banks, which have investors from all over the world.

Alps This magnificent, snow-capped range extends from France, through Switzerland, Austria and northern Italy, into Slovenia. The most famous high peak in the Swiss Alps is the Matterhorn.

 AUSTRIA

Area: 32,378sq miles (83,859sq km)
Highest point: Gross Glockner 12,457ft (3,797m)
Population: 8,193,000
Capital and largest city: Vienna (pop 2,179,000)
Other large cities: Graz (226,000)
Official language: German
Religion: Christianity (Roman Catholic 74%)
Government: Federal republic
Currency: Euro

 SWITZERLAND

Area: 15,940sq miles (41,284sq km)
Highest point: Dufourspitze of Monte Rosa 15,203ft (4,634m)
Population: 7,524,000
Capital: Bern (pop 129,000)
Largest cities: Zurich (939,000)
Geneva (399,000)
Basel (176,000)
Official languages: French, German, Italian
Religion: Christianity (Roman Catholic 46%, Protestant 40%)
Government: Federal republic
Currency: Swiss franc

Watches and precision instruments are famous Swiss products. Switzerland lacks natural resources. Its skilled workers use imported materials to make valuable products.

Postage stamps provide a useful source of income for Liechtenstein. Many stamps prized by collectors show paintings that belong to the country's prince.

 LIECHTENSTEIN

Area: 62sq miles (160sq km)
Population: 34,000
Capital: Vaduz (pop 5,000)
Official language: German
Religion: Christianity (Roman Catholic 76%)
Government: Monarchy (principality)
Currency: Swiss franc

Lake Constance

Rhine

Basel • Winterthur• Konstanz

Aarau • **Zurich** Sankt Gallen • Dornbirn

Zurichsee

Lucerne • Vaduz St Anton

Neuchâtel • Bern **LIECHTENSTEIN**

Lake Neuchâtel Chur

Rhine L

SWITZERLAND A

Lausanne St Moritz

Lake Geneva Locarno

Geneva Rhône Lake Maggiore Lugano

Matterhorn 14,692ft (4,478m) Zermatt

Monte Rosa 15,203ft (4,634m)

0   100 miles

0   100 kilometers

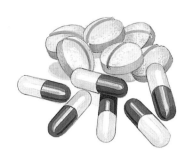

Pharmaceuticals (chemicals used in medicine) are made in both Austria and Switzerland. Austria produces many luxury goods, such as fine glassware and jewelry, but metals and metal goods are the chief products and exports.

Wolfgang Amadeus Mozart (1756-91) was born in Salzburg, Austria, and started to compose and perform as a child. He was one of the greatest of all musical geniuses. Other great Austrian composers include Joseph Haydn, Franz Schubert and Gustav Mahler.

Edelweiss is a plant with white, star-shaped flowers that grows in the Alps. The upper parts of the Alps are treeless and the vegetation resembles that of the tundra in the Arctic regions of northern Europe.

Krems

Vienna

Linz

Danube

Sankt Pölten

Lake Neusiedler

Wels

Steyr

Wiener Neustadt

Enns

Salzburg

A U S T R I A

Leoben

Inn

Salzach

Graz

Innsbruck

S

Mur

Gross Glockner 12,457ft (3,797m)

P

Villach

Klagenfurt

Skiing is a popular winter sport in the Alps. St Moritz and Zermatt are major resorts in Switzerland, while St Anton has some of the world's most challenging ski slopes. Austrian resorts include Innsbruck and Salzburg.

FRANCE

France is the largest country in western Europe. It has a beautiful landscape and fine cities with many historic buildings. It is also one of the world's top manufacturing nations and Paris is a world center of the fashion industry. Agriculture employs only three percent of the population, but France is western Europe's leading producer of farm products. France is famous for its excellent food and wines, and is one of the most prosperous countries in Europe.

Charles de Gaulle (1890-1970) led the French resistance to Germany in World War II. As France's president (1958-69), he tackled the problems arising from the granting of independence to France's overseas empire.

FRANCE

Area: 212,935sq miles (551,500sq km)
Highest point: Mont Blanc 15,771ft (4,807m)
Population: 60,876,000
Capital and largest city: Paris (pop 9,794,000)
Other large cities: Lyon (1,362,000)
Marseille (1,357,000)
Lille (1,007,000)
Nice (889,000)
Toulouse (761,000)
Bordeaux (754,000)
Nantes (545,000)
Strasbourg (427,000)
Official language: French
Religions: Christianity (Roman Catholic 85%), Islam 7%
Government: Republic
Currency: Euro

MONACO

Area: 0.6sq miles (1.5sq km)
Population: 33,000
Capital: Monaco (1,100)
Official language: French
Religion: Christianity (Roman Catholic 90%)
Government: Monarchy under French protection
Currency: Euro

Eiffel Tower This wrought-iron tower in Paris is the city's most famous landmark. It was built for the World Fair of 1889. Paris is a great center of the arts and education, and also a major industrial city.

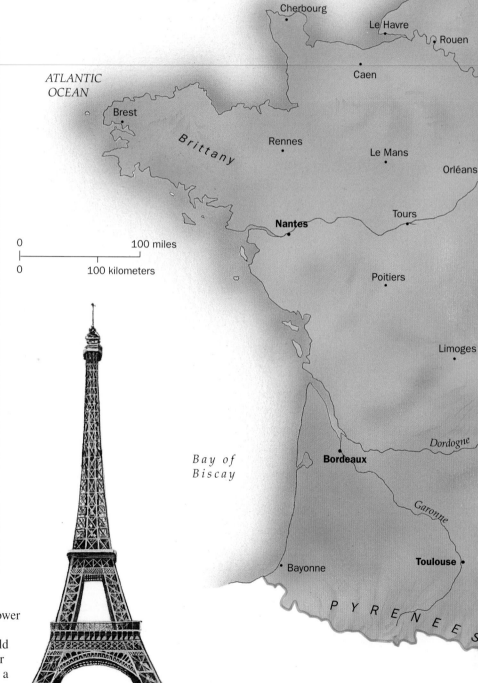

ATLANTIC
OCEAN

Calais

English Channel

Cherbourg

Le Havre

Rouen

Caen

Brest

Brittany

Rennes

Le Mans

Orléans

Nantes

Tours

0   100 miles

0   100 kilometers

Poitiers

Limoges

Bay of
Biscay

Dordogne

Bordeaux

Garonne

Toulouse

Bayonne

P Y R E N E E S

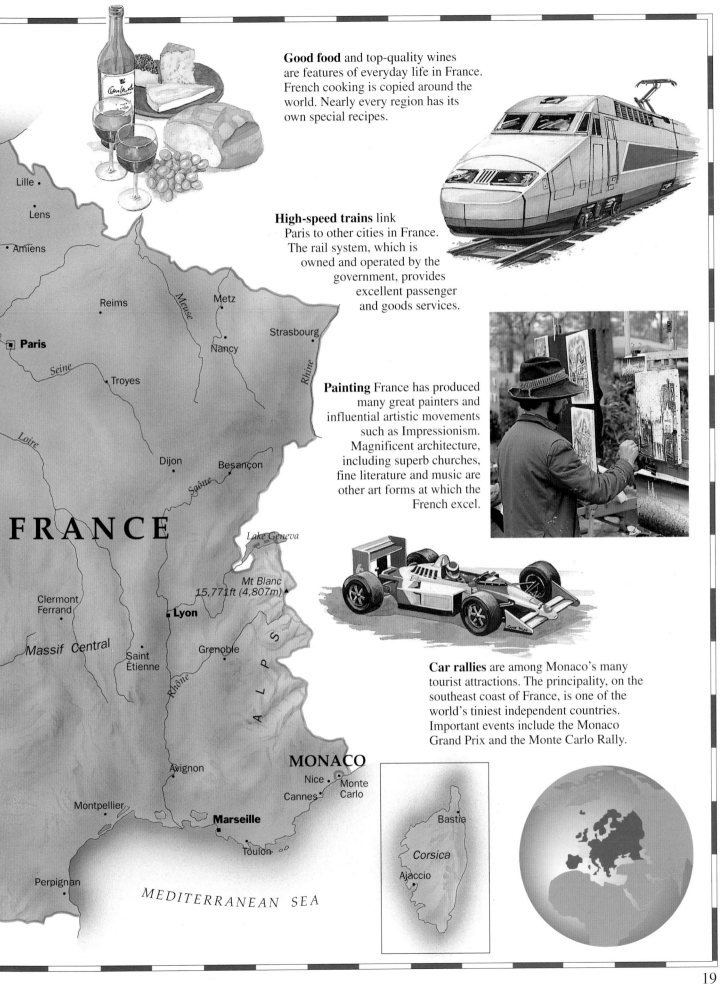

Good food and top-quality wines are features of everyday life in France. French cooking is copied around the world. Nearly every region has its own special recipes.

High-speed trains link Paris to other cities in France. The rail system, which is owned and operated by the government, provides excellent passenger and goods services.

Painting France has produced many great painters and influential artistic movements such as Impressionism. Magnificent architecture, including superb churches, fine literature and music are other art forms at which the French excel.

Car rallies are among Monaco's many tourist attractions. The principality, on the southeast coast of France, is one of the world's tiniest independent countries. Important events include the Monaco Grand Prix and the Monte Carlo Rally.

Lille
Lens
Amiens
Reims
Metz
Strasbourg
Nancy
Paris
Seine
Troyes
Meuse
Rhine
Loire
Dijon
Besançon
Saône
FRANCE
Lake Geneva
Mt Blanc
15,771ft (4,807m)
Clermont Ferrand
Lyon
Massif Central
Saint Étienne
Grenoble
ALPS
Rhône
Avignon
MONACO
Montpellier
Nice
Monte Carlo
Cannes
Marseille
Toulon
Perpignan
MEDITERRANEAN SEA

Bastia
Corsica
Ajaccio

IBERIAN PENINSULA

The Iberian Peninsula consists of two large countries, Spain and Portugal, together with the tiny state of Andorra, in the Pyrenees Mountains in the northeast, and Gibraltar, a small British territory, in the far south. The Canary Islands off the coast of Africa also belong to Spain.

Spain is western Europe's second largest country after France. Spain's economy was shattered by a civil war (1936-39), but since the 1950s it has developed into a fairly prosperous nation. Portugal was a dictatorship from 1933 until 1968. Since 1968, its economy has grown, but it remains one of the poorer members of the European Union.

 SPAIN

Area: 195,365sq miles (505,992sq km)
Highest point: Pico de Teide, in the Canary Islands, 12,198ft (3,718m)
Population: 40,000,000
Capital and largest city: Madrid (pop 5,103,000)
Other large cities: Barcelona (4,378,000) Valencia (754,000)
Languages: Castilian Spanish (official), Catalan, Galician, Basque
Religion: Christianity (Roman Catholic 94%)
Government: Monarchy
Currency: Euro

 PORTUGAL

Area: 35,514sq miles (91,982sq km)
Highest point: Estrela, 6,539ft (1,993m)
Population: 10,606,000
Capital and largest city: Lisbon (pop 1,962,000)
Other large cities: Oporto (1,254,000)
Official language: Portuguese
Religion: Christianity (Roman Catholic 94%)
Government: Republic
Currency: Euro

 ANDORRA

Area: 175sq miles (453sq km)
Highest point: Coma Pedrosa 9,665ft (2,946m)
Population: 71,000
Capital: Andorra La Vella (pop 21,000)
Official language: Catalan
Religion: Christianity (Roman Catholic 92%)
Government: Principality
Currency: Euro

Bay of Biscay

Gijón
Santander
La Coruña
Oviedo
Santiago de Compostela
Cantabrian Mts
León
Vigo
Orense
Burgos
ATLANTIC OCEAN
Braga
Valladolid
Duero
Oporto
Douro
Salamanca
Estrela 6,539ft (1,993m)
Coimbra
Madrid
PORTUGAL
Tajo (Tagus)
Toledo
Cáceres
S P A I N
Guadiana
Lisbon
Setúbal
Badajoz
Evora
Linares
Guadalqui
Córdoba
Huelva
Seville
Lagos
Granada
Sierra
Faro
Jerez de la Frontera
Málaga
Cadiz
Gibraltar (UK)

0 — 100 miles
0 — 100 kilometers

Canary Islands (Spain)
ATLANTIC OCEAN
La Palma
Lanzarote
Tenerife
Santa Cruz
Gomera
Las Palmas
Fuerteventura
Pico de Teide 12,198ft (3,718m)
Hierro
Gran Canaria

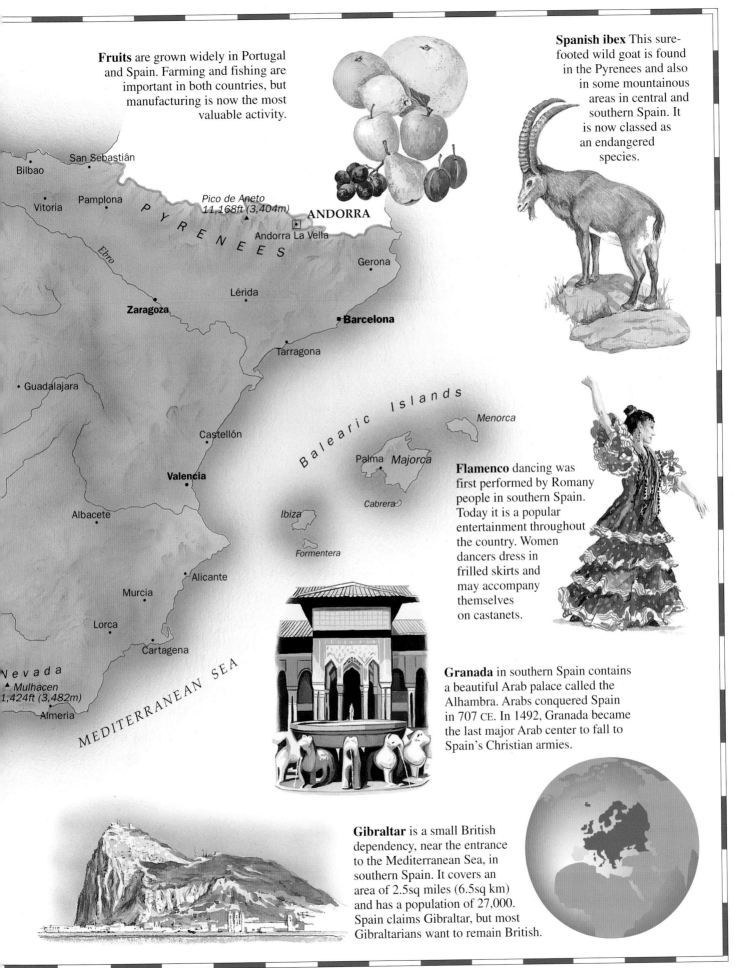

Fruits are grown widely in Portugal and Spain. Farming and fishing are important in both countries, but manufacturing is now the most valuable activity.

Spanish ibex This sure-footed wild goat is found in the Pyrenees and also in some mountainous areas in central and southern Spain. It is now classed as an endangered species.

Bilbao

San Sebastián

Vitoria

Pamplona

P Y R E N E E S

Pico de Aneto 11,168ft (3,404m)

ANDORRA

Andorra La Vella

Gerona

Ebro

Lérida

Zaragoza

Barcelona

Tarragona

Guadalajara

B a l e a r i c   I s l a n d s

Menorca

Castellón

Palma   *Majorca*

Valencia

Cabrera

Albacete

Ibiza

Formentera

Flamenco dancing was first performed by Romany people in southern Spain. Today it is a popular entertainment throughout the country. Women dancers dress in frilled skirts and may accompany themselves on castanets.

Alicante

Murcia

Lorca

Cartagena

N e v a d a

Mulhacen 11,424ft (3,482m)

Almeria

M E D I T E R R A N E A N   S E A

Granada in southern Spain contains a beautiful Arab palace called the Alhambra. Arabs conquered Spain in 707 CE. In 1492, Granada became the last major Arab center to fall to Spain's Christian armies.

Gibraltar is a small British dependency, near the entrance to the Mediterranean Sea, in southern Spain. It covers an area of 2.5sq miles (6.5sq km) and has a population of 27,000. Spain claims Gibraltar, but most Gibraltarians want to remain British.

ITALY

Italy extends like a leg and foot into the Mediterranean Sea. The Alps in the far north overlook the fertile River Po basin, where most of Italy's major industrial cities are situated. The "leg" of Italy contains the Apennine Mountains and, in the southwest, are some active volcanoes, including Etna on the island of Sicily.

Two tiny independent nations lie inside Italy. They are San Marino and Vatican City, which covers an area about the size of a town park in the city of Rome. South of Sicily is the island nation of Malta.

ITALY

Area: 116,320sq miles (301,268sq km)
Highest point: Mont Blanc 15,771ft (4,807m)
Population: 58,134,000
Capital: Rome (pop 2,665,000)
Other large cities: Milan (4,183,000)
Naples (2,995,000)
Turin (1,247,000)
Official language: Italian
Religion: Christianity (Roman Catholic 90%)
Government: Republic
Currency: Euro

MALTA

Area: 122sq miles (316sq km)
Population: 400,000
Capital: Valletta (pop 83,000)
Official languages: Maltese, English
Religion: Christianity (Roman Catholic 98%)
Government: Republic
Currency: Maltese lira

SAN MARINO

Area: 24sq miles (61sq km)
Population: 29,000
Capital: San Marino (pop 4,500)
Official language: Italian
Religion: Christianity (Roman Catholic 90%)
Government: Republic
Currency: Euro

VATICAN CITY

Area: 0.17sq miles (0.44sq km)
Population: 900
Government: Papacy
Currency: Euro

Rome The Colosseum, a huge amphitheater dedicated in 79 CE, is one of many famous ruins of the Roman Empire. Roman citizens gathered there to watch state-run spectacles, including fights between gladiators and wild animals.

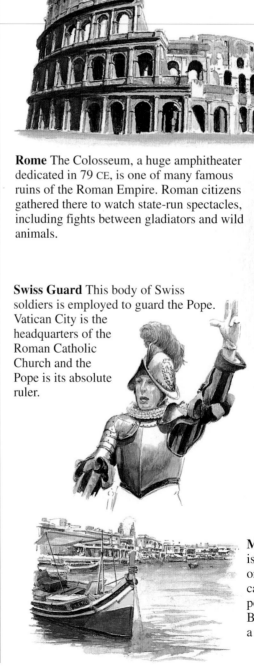

Swiss Guard This body of Swiss soldiers is employed to guard the Pope. Vatican City is the headquarters of the Roman Catholic Church and the Pope is its absolute ruler.

Malta consists of several islands south of Sicily. Valletta, on the largest island, which is also called Malta, is the capital and chief port. Malta became independent from Britain in 1964, though Britain had a naval base there until 1979.

Venice is a city built on about 120 islands in the Adriatic Sea. Its streets are canals lined with beautiful buildings that are increasingly threatened by flooding, pollution and overcrowding by tourists. Italy's cities, historic sites and beautiful beaches attract about 40 million tourists to the country each year.

Style Elegant fashions and stylish cars are products that have given Italy its worldwide reputation for excellence in design. Around 50 years ago, Italy was mainly a farming country, but it has grown increasingly rich through manufacturing.

Garibaldi (1807-82) Giuseppe Garibaldi was a military hero who fought to unite Italy. In 1860, with the help of 1,000 volunteers known, as *red shirts*, he conquered Sicily.

Pompeii is an ancient Roman town near Naples. In 79 CE it was buried by volcanic ash that erupted from nearby Mount Vesuvius. The volcano has erupted many times since, the last time in 1944.

Map labels

Bolzano
Trento
Udine
Treviso
Verona · Venice · Trieste
Padova
Adige
Modena
Bologna · Ravenna
San Marino · Rimini
SAN MARINO
Florence
Perugia · Assisi
Arno
Tiber
Rome
VATICAN CITY
ITALY
Ancona
Pescara
Adriatic Sea
Foggia
Bari
Naples · Vesuvius · Pompeii
Salerno · Potenza
Brindisi
Taranto
Tyrrhenian Sea
Catanzaro
Ustica
Lipari Is
Palermo · Messina
Trapani · Reggio di Calabria
Etna 10,958ft (3,340m)
Sicily · Catania
Licata
Pantelleria
MALTA · Valletta

0   100 miles
0   100 kilometers

GREECE AND THE BALKANS

This region in southeastern Europe includes Greece, the center of a great ancient civilization, Albania, and six countries that, until the early 1990s, made up the Communist country of Yugoslavia. Following the break-up of Yugoslavia, civil wars in Bosnia and Herzegovina, Croatia and in the Kosovo region of Serbia caused great damage and loss of life. The region's land is mostly rugged. Farming is important, but manufacturing is the most valuable activity.

GREECE

Area: 50,949sq miles (131,957sq km)
Population: 10,688,000
Capital: Athens (pop 3,215,000)
Official language: Greek
Religion: Christianity (Greek Orthodox 98%)
Government: Republic
Currency: Euro

SLOVENIA

Area: 7,821sq miles (20,256sq km)
Population: 2,010,000
Capital: Ljubljana (pop 256,000)
Official language: Slovene
Religion: Christianity (Roman Catholic 58%)
Government: Republic
Currency: Tolar

CROATIA

Area: 34,022sq miles (88,117sq km)
Population: 4,495,000
Capital: Zagreb (pop 688,000)
Official language: Croatian (Serbo-Croatian)
Religion: Christianity (Roman Catholic 87%)
Government: Republic
Currency: Kuna

BOSNIA AND HERZEGOVINA

Area: 19,741sq miles (51,129sq km)
Population: 4,499,000
Capital: Sarajevo (pop 579,000)
Official language: Bosnian (Serbo-Croatian)
Religions: Christianity 46%, Islam 40%
Currency: Marka

MONTENEGRO

Area: 5,333sq miles (13,812sq km)
Population: 631,000
Capital: Podgorica (pop 152,000)
Official language: Montenegrin (Serbian)
Religions: Orthodox 69%, Islam 19%
Currency: Euro

ALBANIA

Area: 11,100sq miles (28,748sq km)
Population: 3,582,000
Capital: Tirana (pop 367,000)
Official language: Albanian
Religions: Islam, Christianity
Government: Republic
Currency: Lek

MACEDONIA

Area: 9,928sq miles (25,713sq km)
Population: 2,051,000
Capital: Skopje (pop 447,000)
Official language: Macedonian
Religions: Serbian (Macedonian) Orthodox 64%, Islam 33%
Government: Republic
Currency: Denar

SERBIA

Area: 34,116sq miles (88,361sq km)
Population: 9,396,000
Capital: Belgrade (pop 1,118,000)
Official language: Serbian (Serbo-Croatian)
Religions: Serbian Orthodox 65%, Islam 19%
Government: Republic
Currency: New dinar

Danube The middle course of this important river forms part of the boundary of Croatia. It then flows across northern Serbia. Belgrade stands at the point where the river joins the Sava, one of its main tributaries.

Marshal Tito (1892-1980) After World War II, Tito (real name, Josip Broz) served as president of Communist Yugoslavia. He kept the country united. After his death, conflict began between various language and religious groups, which led to a violent break-up of the country.

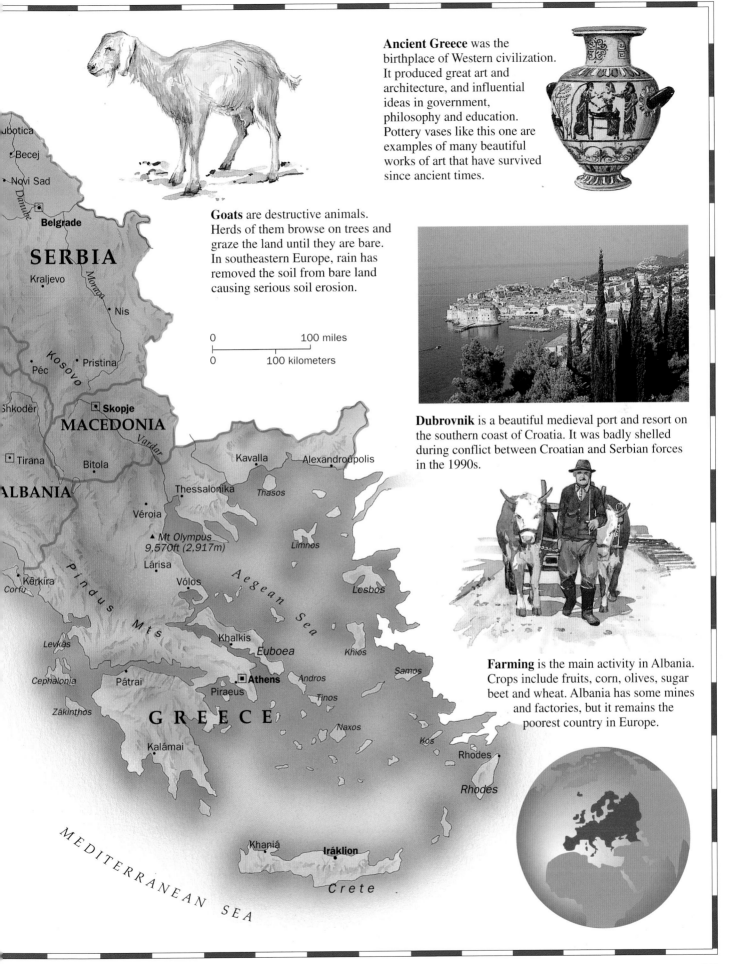

Ancient Greece was the birthplace of Western civilization. It produced great art and architecture, and influential ideas in government, philosophy and education. Pottery vases like this one are examples of many beautiful works of art that have survived since ancient times.

Goats are destructive animals. Herds of them browse on trees and graze the land until they are bare. In southeastern Europe, rain has removed the soil from bare land causing serious soil erosion.

0   100 miles
0   100 kilometers

Dubrovnik is a beautiful medieval port and resort on the southern coast of Croatia. It was badly shelled during conflict between Croatian and Serbian forces in the 1990s.

Farming is the main activity in Albania. Crops include fruits, corn, olives, sugar beet and wheat. Albania has some mines and factories, but it remains the poorest country in Europe.

ubotica
• Becej
• Novi Sad
Danube
□ **Belgrade**
SERBIA
• Kraljevo
Morava
• Nis
Kosovo
• Pristina
• Péc
hkodër
□ **Skopje**
MACEDONIA
Vardar
□ • Tirana
Bitola
LBANIA
Kavalla • Alexandroúpolis
Thessaloníka
Thasos
• Véroia
▲ *Mt Olympus*
9,570ft (2,917m)
• Lárisa
Aegean Sea
Limnos
• Vólos
Kêrkira
Corfu
Pindus Mts
Lesbos
Levkás
Khalkís
Euboea
Khíos
Cephalonia
• Pátrai
□ ■ **Athens**
Andros
Samos
Piraeus
Zákinthos
G R E E C E
Tinos
Naxos
• Kalámai
Kos
Rhodes
Rhodes
M E D I T E R R A N E A N   S E A
Khaniá
Iráklion
Crete

25

EAST-CENTRAL EUROPE

East-central Europe includes Poland, which faces the Baltic Sea. It also includes the landlocked Czech Republic and Slovakia, which until December 31, 1992, formed a single country, Czechoslovakia.

These countries had Communist governments from 1948 until the early 1990s when Communist policies were abandoned. In the 1990s, they faced many problems as they restored the land and government-owned industries to private ownership. All three nations became members of the European Union in 2004.

POLAND

Area: 124,808sq miles (323,250sq km)
Highest point: Rysy Peak 8,199ft (2,499m)
Population: 38,537,000
Capital: Warsaw (pop 2,200,000)
Other large cities: Katowice (3,069,000)
Lódz (974,000)
Kraków (859,000)
Official language: Polish
Religion: Christianity (Roman Catholic 90%)
Government: Republic
Currency: Zloty

CZECH REPUBLIC

Area: 30,450sq miles (78,864sq km)
Highest point: Snezka, in the Sudeten Mountains, 5,256ft (1,602m)
Population: 10,235,000
Capital and largest city: Prague (pop 1,170,000)
Other large cities: Brno (371,000)
Ostrava (314,000)
Official language: Czech
Religion: Christianity (Roman Catholic 26%)
Government: Republic
Currency: Czech koruna

SLOVAKIA

Area: 18,924sq miles (49,012sq km)
Highest point: Gerlachovsky Stit 8,711ft (2,655m)
Population: 5,439,000
Capital and largest city: Bratislava (pop 425,000)
Other large cities: Kosice (236,000)
Presov (93,000)
Official language: Slovak
Religion: Christianity (Roman Catholic 69%)
Government: Republic
Currency: Slovak koruna

Prague, the capital of former Czechoslovakia, became the capital of the Czech Republic when Czechoslovakia split apart on January 1, 1993. It is one of the most beautiful cities in eastern Europe.

European bison These animals were once common in Europe, but few now remain. A small herd is protected in the forested Bialowieza National Park, which lies partly in Poland and partly in Belarus.

BALTIC SEA

Koszalin
Szczecinek
Szczecin
Bydgoszcz
Pila
Gorzów Wielkopolski
Warta
Poznan
P
Neisse
Zielona Góra
Wroclaw
Oder
Sudeten Mts
Walbrzych
Liberec
Snezka 5,256ft (1,602m)
Nysa
Ústi nád Labem
Ore Mts
Elbe
Prague
CZECH REPUBLIC
Prostejov
Plzen
Vltava
Jihlava
Brno
Ceske Budejovice
Bratislava

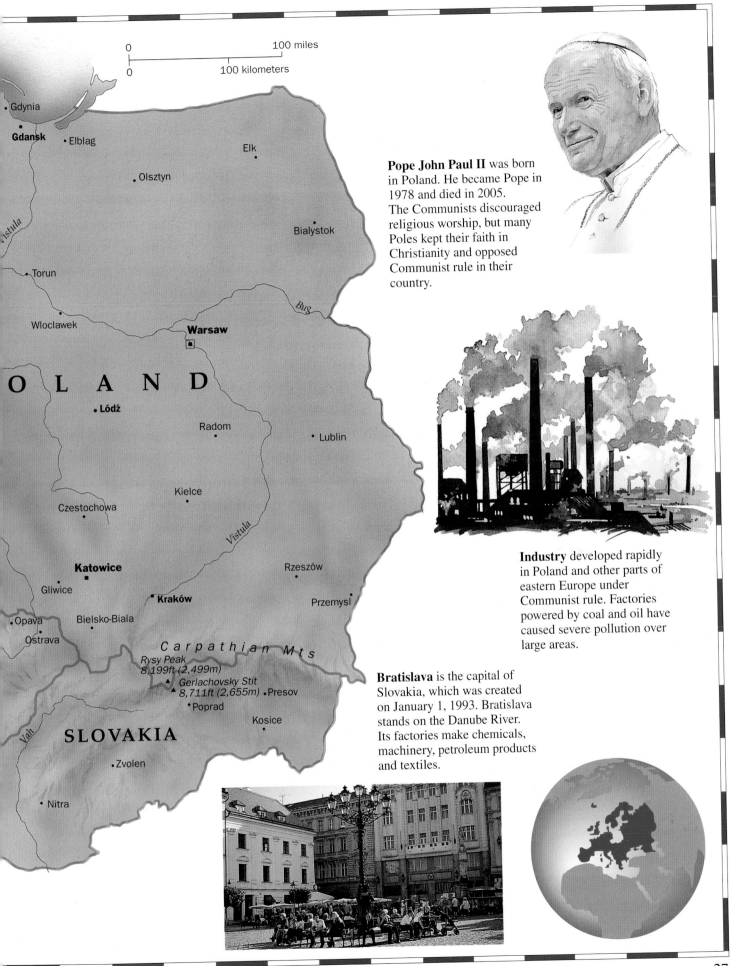

0
100 miles

0
100 kilometers

Gdynia

Gdansk • Elblag

Elk

• Olsztyn

Bialystok

Vistula

• Torun

Bug

• Wloclawek

Warsaw

P O L A N D

• **Lódź**

Radom

• Lublin

Kielce

Czestochowa

Vistula

Katowice

Rzeszów

Gliwice

Kraków

Przemysl

• Opava

Bielsko-Biala

Ostrava

C a r p a t h i a n   M t s

Rysy Peak
8,199ft (2,499m)

Gerlachovsky Stit
8,711ft (2,655m) • Presov

• Poprad

Kosice

SLOVAKIA

Vah

• Zvolen

• Nitra

Pope John Paul II was born
in Poland. He became Pope in
1978 and died in 2005.
The Communists discouraged
religious worship, but many
Poles kept their faith in
Christianity and opposed
Communist rule in their
country.

Industry developed rapidly
in Poland and other parts of
eastern Europe under
Communist rule. Factories
powered by coal and oil have
caused severe pollution over
large areas.

Bratislava is the capital of
Slovakia, which was created
on January 1, 1993. Bratislava
stands on the Danube River.
Its factories make chemicals,
machinery, petroleum products
and textiles.

SOUTHEASTERN EUROPE

Southeastern Europe contains landlocked Hungary and two countries, Romania and Bulgaria, which have coastlines on the Black Sea. All three countries had mainly agricultural economies until they came under Communist rule in the late 1940s. Today manufacturing is the most valuable activity. In the 1990s, the countries overcame problems as they worked to restore democracy and private ownership of all economic activity. Hungary joined the European Union in 2004, and the other two countries in 2007.

Lake Neusiedler

Salgotarján
Miskolc
Nyíregyháza
Sopron
Győr
Kekes 3,330ft (1,015m)
Tisza
■ **Budapest**
Pápa
Székesfehérvar
Debrecen
Cegléd
Zalaegerszeg
Lake Balaton
HUNGARY
Kecskemét
Oradea
Danube
Kaposvár
Arad
Pécs
Timisoara
Lugoj
Resita

HUNGARY

Area: 35,920sq miles (93,032sq km)
Highest point: Mount Kekes 3,330ft (1,015m)
Population: 9,981,000
Capital and largest city: Budapest (pop 1,708,000)
Other large cities: Debrecen (206,000) Miskolc (180,000)
Official language: Hungarian
Religion: Christianity (Roman Catholic 51%, Protestant 20%)
Government: Republic
Currency: Forint

ROMANIA

Area: 92,043sq miles (238,391sq km)
Highest point: Mount Moldoveanu 8,343ft (2,543m)
Population: 22,304,000
Capital and largest city: Bucharest (pop 1,853,000)
Other large cities: Constanta (310,000) Iasi (340,000)
Official language: Romanian
Religion: Christianity (Eastern Orthodox 90%)
Government: Republic
Currency: New Leu

BULGARIA

Area: 42,823sq miles (110,912sq km)
Highest point: Musala Peak 9,596ft (2,925m)
Population: 7,385,000
Capital and largest city: Sofia (pop 1,076,000)
Other large cities: Plovdiv (338,000) Varna (321,000)
Official language: Bulgarian
Religions: Christianity (Bulgarian Orthodox 84%), Islam 12%
Government: Republic
Currency: Lev

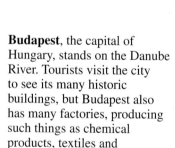

Wheat is the leading grain crop in southeastern Europe. Corn is also important. Other food crops include fruits, potatoes, sugar beet and various vegetables.

Budapest, the capital of Hungary, stands on the Danube River. Tourists visit the city to see its many historic buildings, but Budapest also has many factories, producing such things as chemical products, textiles and transport equipment.

Wild boars were once common in the forests of central Europe. But most of the original forests have been cut down to make way for farms and cities. Wild boars, along with many other plant and animal species, are now rare.

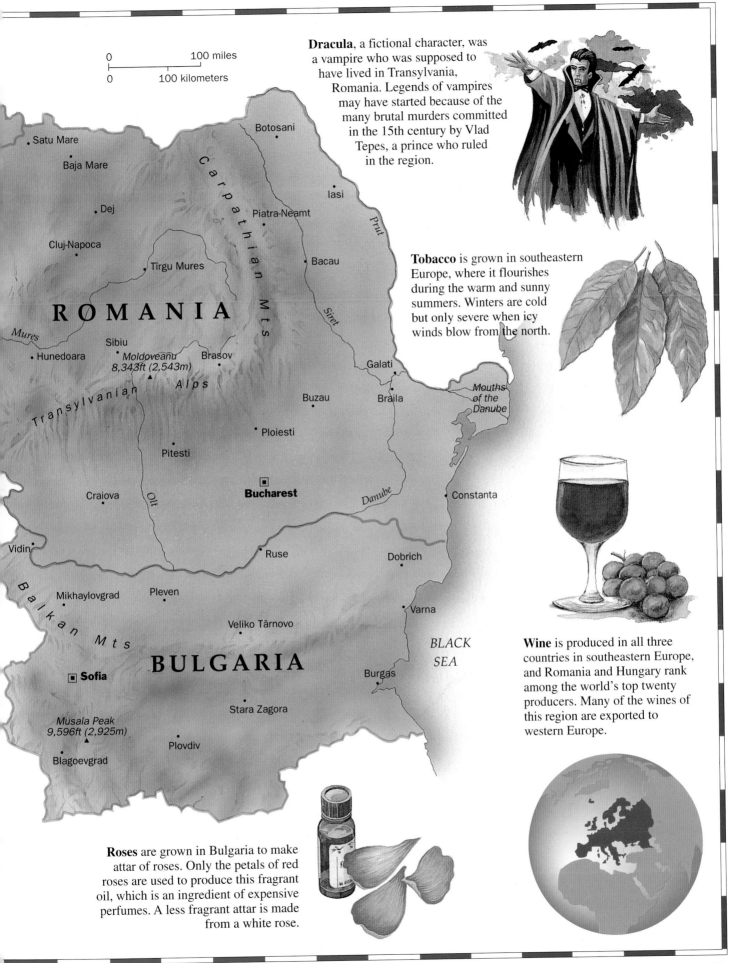

Dracula, a fictional character, was a vampire who was supposed to have lived in Transylvania, Romania. Legends of vampires may have started because of the many brutal murders committed in the 15th century by Vlad Tepes, a prince who ruled in the region.

Tobacco is grown in southeastern Europe, where it flourishes during the warm and sunny summers. Winters are cold but only severe when icy winds blow from the north.

Wine is produced in all three countries in southeastern Europe, and Romania and Hungary rank among the world's top twenty producers. Many of the wines of this region are exported to western Europe.

Roses are grown in Bulgaria to make attar of roses. Only the petals of red roses are used to produce this fragrant oil, which is an ingredient of expensive perfumes. A less fragrant attar is made from a white rose.

0 — 100 miles
0 — 100 kilometers

Satu Mare
Baja Mare
Dej
Cluj-Napoca
Botosani
Iasi
Piatra-Neamt
Prut
Carpathian Mts
Tirgu Mures
Bacau
Siret
R O M A N I A
Mures
Sibiu
Hunedoara
Moldoveanu
8,343ft (2,543m)
Brasov
Galati
Transylvanian   Alps
Buzau
Braila
Mouths of the Danube
Ploiesti
Pitesti
Craiova
Bucharest
Danube
Constanta
Vidin
Ruse
Dobrich
Mikhaylovgrad
Pleven
Balkan   Mts
Veliko Târnovo
Varna
B U L G A R I A
Sofia
Burgas
BLACK SEA
Musala Peak
9,596ft (2,925m)
Stara Zagora
Plovdiv
Blagoevgrad

EASTERN EUROPE

When the Soviet Union broke up in December 1991, following the collapse of Communism, the 15 republics that made up the Soviet Union became independent nations. The map of eastern Europe shown here contains six of them. In the 1990s, the governments of the new countries worked to set up new democratic political, legal and economic systems. Three of these new democratic countries, Estonia, Latvia and Lithuania, became members of the European Union in 2004.

ESTONIA

Area: 17,413sq miles (45,100sq km)
Population: 1,324,000
Capital: Tallinn (pop 391,000)
Official language: Estonian
Religion: Christianity (28%)
Government: Republic
Currency: Kroon

LATVIA

Area: 24,924sq miles (64,600sq km)
Population: 2,275,000
Capital: Riga (pop 733,000)
Official language: Latvian
Religion: Christianity (40%)
Government: Republic
Currency: Lat

LITHUANIA

Area: 25,174sq miles (65,200sq km)
Population: 3,586,000
Capital: Vilnius (pop 549,000)
Official language: Lithuanian
Religion: Christianity (Roman Catholic 79%)
Government: Republic
Currency: Litas

BELARUS

Area: 80,155sq miles (207,600sq km)
Population: 10,293,000
Capital: Minsk (pop 1,705,000)
Official languages: Belarussian, Russian
Religion: Christianity (Eastern Othodox 80%)
Government: Republic
Currency: Belarussian rouble

UKRAINE

Area: 233,090sq miles (603,700sq km)
Population: 46,711,000
Capital: Kiev (pop 2,618,000)
Official language: Ukrainian
Religion: Christianity (43%)
Government: Republic
Currency: Hryvnia

MOLDOVA

Area: 13,012sq miles (33,700sq km)
Population: 4,467,000
Capital: Chisinau (pop 662,000)
Official language: Romanian
Religion: Christianity (Eastern Orthodox 98%)
Government: Republic
Currency: Moldovan leu

Ukraine has been called the breadbasket of Europe because of the amount of wheat it grows on its vast plains. It also ranks as one of the world's top producers of sugar beet. Wheat is grown throughout eastern Europe.

Amber is the hardened resin of ancient pine trees that grew in northern Europe millions of years ago. A large amount is found along the Baltic Sea coasts of Estonia, Latvia and Lithuania. It is used in jewelry.

0 ——————— 100 miles
0 ——————— 100 kilometers

Chernobyl, near Kiev in Ukraine, was the site of the worst nuclear accident in history. An explosion at its nuclear power plant in 1986 released radioactive substances into the atmosphere, which were carried by winds into northern and western Europe.

Riga is the capital of Latvia. It stands on the Gulf of Riga and has beautiful medieval buildings. It is also a major industrial city, producing chemicals, electronics and machinery.

Vitsyebsk

Mahilyow

Babruysk

Homyel

Chernobyl

Wolves, which are one of the ancestors of domestic dogs, are found throughout eastern Europe. They live mostly in open country where there is cover. Their numbers have been greatly reduced by hunting.

■ **Kiev**

U K R A I N E

■ **Kharkov**

Poltava

Luhansk

Kramatorsk

Horlivka

Dneprodzerzinsk

Dnepropetrovsk

• Makiyivka

Kryvyy Rih •

Zaporozje

Donetsk

Mariupol'

Kherson   *Dnepr*

Melitopol

Odessa

Sea of Azov

Flax is a leading crop in Belarus and Ukraine. These two countries are among the world's top ten producers. Flax fiber is used to make linen, and the seeds to make linseed oil.

Simferopol'

Sevastopol

B l a c k   S e a

EUROPEAN RUSSIA

Only part of Russia, the world's largest country, is in Europe. The rest is in Asia. Russia had a troubled history in the 20th century. In 1917, Communists took power. From 1922, Russia became the major part of the vast Soviet Union. In World War II (1939-45), German forces invaded European Russia and caused great destruction. In 1991, after Communism had failed to solve the country's problems, the Soviet Union broke up into 15 countries. The largest of these is Russia.

RUSSIA

Area: 6,592,850sq miles (17,075,400sq km), of which about 25% is in Europe
Highest point: Mount Elbrus, in the Caucasus Mountains, 18,510ft (5,642m)
Population: 142,894,000 (about 80% of whom live in European Russia)
Capital and largest city: Moscow (pop 10,469,000)
Other large cities (in European Russia):
St Petersburg (5,214,000)
Nizhniy Novgorod (1,331,000)
Samara (1,260,000)
Kazan (1,100,000)
Official language: Russian
Religions: Christianity (Russian Orthodox 16%), Islam 10%
Government: Republic
Currency: Rouble

ASIAN RUSSIA
Asian Russia is thinly populated.
Though three-quarters of Russia is in Asia, it contains only 20 percent of Russia's people.

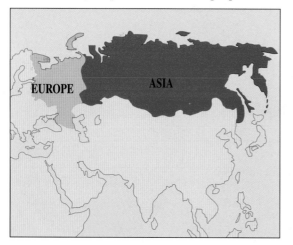

Hammer and sickle
This Communist symbol appeared in yellow on the red flag that was used by the former Soviet Union. It represented the nation's industrial and agricultural workers.

Vladimir Lenin
(1870-1924) founded the Russian Communist Party and led the revolution in 1917 that made Russia a Communist country.

Icons are religious paintings found in Eastern Orthodox churches. The Communists discouraged religious worship, but Christianity survived. The Russian Orthodox Church is the largest religious denomination in Russia.

Murmansk

Wh

Lake Onega

Lake Ladoga

Gulf of Finland

St Petersburg

Cherepovets

Novgorod

Moscow ▪

Kaluga

Tula

Smolensk

0   200 miles
0   200 kilometers

Sea of Azov

Black

Ballet is one of Russia's major art forms. The Kirov Ballet of St Petersburg and the Bolshoi Theatre Ballet in Moscow are world famous. Russian composers include Nikolai Rimsky-Korsakov, Peter Ilich Tchaikovsky and Igor Stravinsky.

Barents Sea

Vorkuta •

Pechora

Mt Narodnaya
6,214ft (1,894m)

• Archangel'sk

Ukhta •

Northern Dvina

• Kotlas

Ural Mountains

RUSSIA

Vologda •

Kirov

Perm

Izhevsk

Yaroslavl

Nizhniy Novgorod   **Kazan**   Kama

Volga

Ufa

• **Ryazan**

Magnitogorsk

Samara

Penza   Syzran

Orenburg

Ural

Saratov

• **Voronezh**

Don

Volgograd

Volga

• **Rostov**

Astrakhan

Caspian Sea

• Krasnodar   • Stavropol'

Caucasus

Sochi •

Grozny •

Mt Elbrus
18,510ft (5,642m)

Machachkala •

Sea

Kremlin This ancient fortress in Moscow is Russia's seat of government. The Kremlin also contains many beautiful buildings that are now museums.

Brown bears live in the northern forests of European Russia. Hunting for furs has greatly reduced the numbers of wild animals in Russia, but many species are now protected in nature reserves.

Industry Russia's many resources include coal, oil and many metals. The country has many heavy industries, which, under Communism, were owned by the government. In the 1990s, Russia worked to restore private ownership of the land and industry.

ПЬЗЖ

Cyrillic alphabet Russian is written in the Cyrillic alphabet, which was invented in the 9th century by two Greek missionaries, St Cyril and his brother St Methodius.

PEOPLE AND BELIEFS

Europe is the home of about 11 percent of the world's population.
It ranks third among the continents in population, after Asia and
Africa, which overtook it in the late 1990s. Large parts of
northern Europe contain few people, but the central plains
of Europe and the Mediterranean region contain
some of the most densely populated areas
in the world. Many people live in
huge cities. Europe's largest
cities include Paris,
Moscow, London,
Berlin and Athens.

**Population densities
in Europe**
Number of people
per square kilometer*

- Over 100
- Between 50 and 100
- Between 10 and 50
- Between 1 and 10
- Below 1

■ Cities of more than
1,000,000 people

● Cities of more than
500,000 people

* 1 square kilometer = .4 square mile

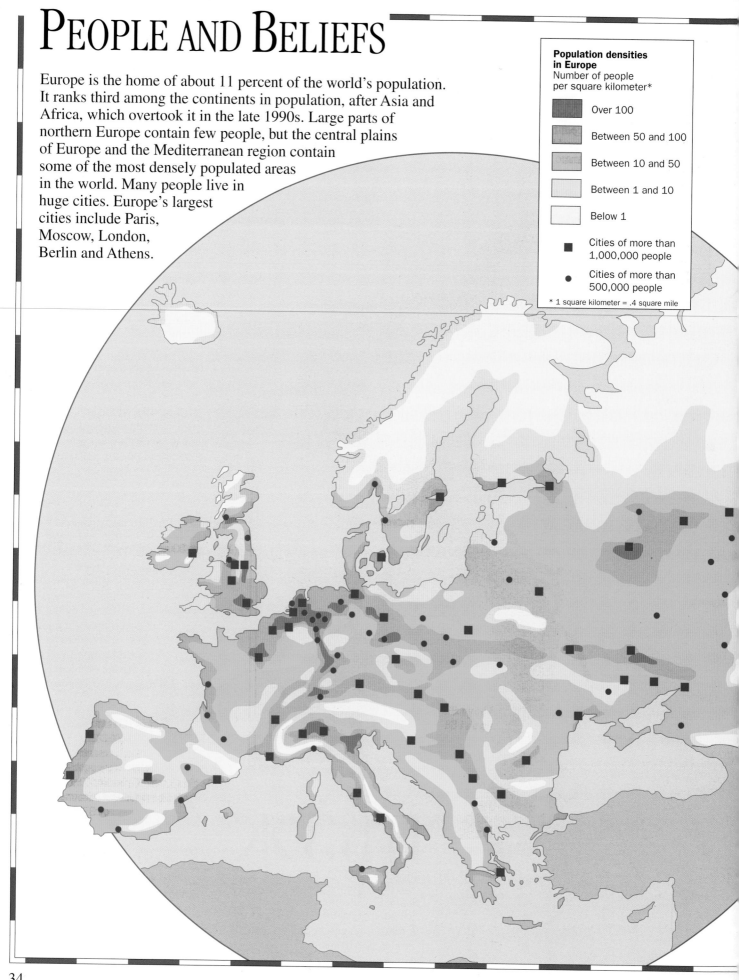

Population and area

Although only 25 percent of Russia lies in Europe, it is by far the largest country in Europe both in area and in population. Ukraine, another country created in 1991 when the Soviet Union broke up, is the second largest country, although in population it ranks sixth.

Germany has the second largest population in Europe, although it ranks only sixth in area. The third most populous European country is the much smaller United Kingdom, which ranks eleventh in area.

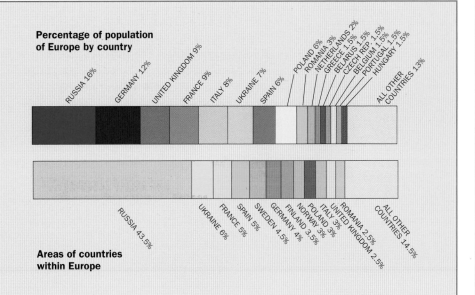

Percentage of population of Europe by country

RUSSIA 16% · GERMANY 12% · UNITED KINGDOM 9% · FRANCE 9% · ITALY 8% · UKRAINE 7% · SPAIN 6% · POLAND 6% · ROMANIA 3% · NETHERLANDS 2% · GREECE 1.5% · BELARUS 1.5% · CZECH REP. 1.5% · BELGIUM 1.5% · PORTUGAL 1.5% · HUNGARY 1.5% · ALL OTHER COUNTRIES 13%

Areas of countries within Europe

RUSSIA 43.5% · UKRAINE 6% · FRANCE 5% · SPAIN 5% · SWEDEN 4.5% · GERMANY 4% · FINLAND 3.5% · NORWAY 3% · POLAND 3% · ITALY 3% · UNITED KINGDOM 2.5% · ROMANIA 2.5% · ALL OTHER COUNTRIES 14.5%

Main religious groups

Christianity, the main religion in Europe, has played an important part in the continent's history, and the great Christian cathedrals testify to its influence on art and architecture.

Roman Catholics make up the largest single group. With their headquarters in Rome, they are strongest in southern Europe and parts of eastern Europe, especially Poland. The other main groups are the Orthodox and the Protestants. Orthodox Christians live chiefly in Greece, the southern nations in eastern Europe and Russia. Protestants live in the northern countries of western Europe. Europe also has Jewish and Islamic communities. Jews live in most parts of Europe, while Muslims live in the Balkans and also in countries, such as France and Germany, which have large numbers of immigrants from North Africa and Southeast Asia.

Under Communism, religious worship was discouraged, but today everyone has freedom of worship. Many people in eastern Europe and elsewhere in Europe do not follow any religion.

Legend:
- Roman Catholic
- Orthodox
- Orthodox and Islamic
- Protestant
- Protestant and Roman Catholic

The great medieval cathedrals of Europe are architectural masterpieces that contain priceless works of art. Thousands of people visit them every year.

CLIMATE AND VEGETATION

Europe's climates range from polar and tundra in the northeast to Mediterranean in the south. The northwest has a mild climate, because temperatures are raised by a warm offshore current, called the North Atlantic Drift – the northern part of the Gulf Stream, which starts in the Gulf of Mexico. Northern Europe has large cold forests of coniferous trees. The natural vegetation of most of central Europe was deciduous forest, with trees that shed their leaves in autumn. Most of this deciduous forest has been cut down to create farmland and space for cities.

Europe's natural vegetation

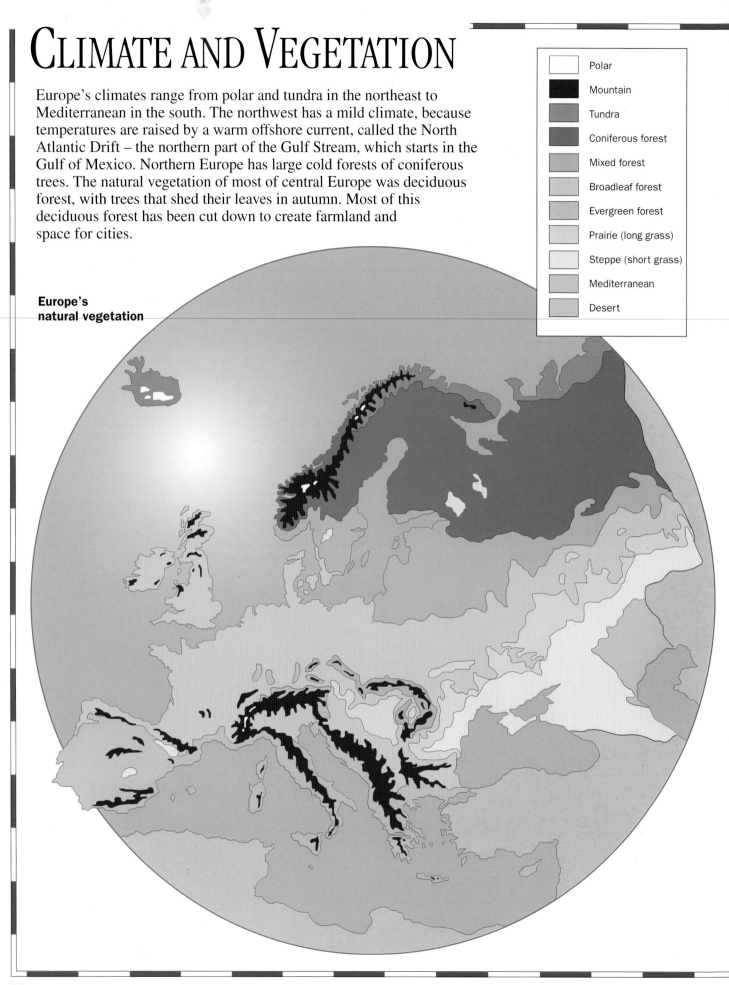

Polar

Mountain

Tundra

Coniferous forest

Mixed forest

Broadleaf forest

Evergreen forest

Prairie (long grass)

Steppe (short grass)

Mediterranean

Desert

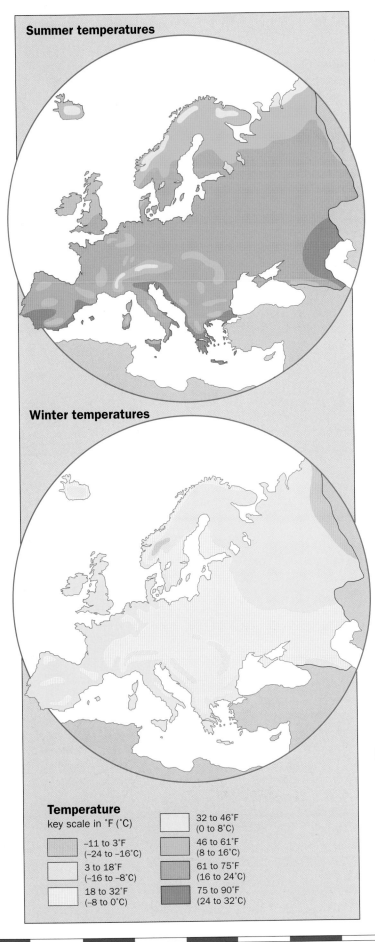

Summer temperatures

Winter temperatures

Range of climates

Europe's climate varies from the cold north to the warm temperate south. The climate also changes from west to east. In the west, the climate is influenced by the Atlantic Ocean. The ocean makes summers milder and winters warmer. To the east, the climate becomes more extreme, with hotter summers and bitterly cold winters. Rainfall in eastern Europe is generally less than in the west.

Ranges of vegetation

The three main types of vegetation in Europe are treeless tundra, forests and grasslands. (Mountains, which get colder with altitude, also have these three types of vegetation.) In the coldest northern regions, summers are short. When the topsoil thaws, low plants grow, providing food for herds of reindeer and other animals. The northern forests contain conifer trees that can survive the cold winters. Farther south are mixed forests of evergreen and deciduous trees. Central and southern Europe have broadleaf forests, containing ash, birch, beech, maple and oak. In the Mediterranean, many trees, including pines, cork oaks and olives, have tough leaves that retain moisture during the hot summers and stay on the trees all year. Grasslands occur in regions with dry climates. The best-known grasslands are in Ukraine and southern European Russia. They are called the steppes.

Annual rainfall
in inches (mm)

Above 59in
(1,500mm)

39 - 59in
(1,000 - 1,500mm)

30 - 39in
(750 - 1,000mm)

20 - 30in
(500 - 750mm)

0 - 20in
(0 - 500mm)

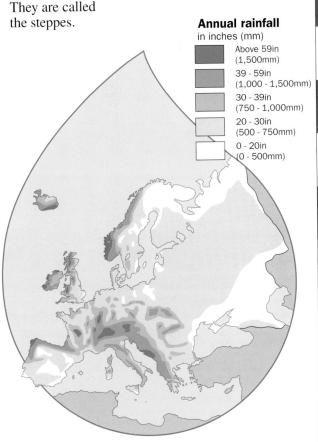

Temperature
key scale in °F (°C)

−11 to 3°F
(−24 to −16°C)

3 to 18°F
(−16 to −8°C)

18 to 32°F
(−8 to 0°C)

32 to 46°F
(0 to 8°C)

46 to 61°F
(8 to 16°C)

61 to 75°F
(16 to 24°C)

75 to 90°F
(24 to 32°C)

ECOLOGY AND ENVIRONMENT

Europe is a prosperous continent, but economic development has caused great damage to the environment. Farming has destroyed natural habitats, harming wildlife. Industry has also caused pollution – in the air, rivers and seas, and also on land – and contributed to global warming. Pollution from one country often spreads to others. Today, the governments of most European countries are working to prevent further damage.

Seals have suffered greatly in recent years from oil spills and the dumping of toxic wastes.

ICELAND

NORWAY

FINLAND

Oil spills

SWEDEN

ESTONIA

LATVIA

RUSSIA

IRELAND

UNITED KINGDOM

DENMARK

LITHUANIA

KALININGRAD (RUSSIA)

Oil spills

Flood

NETHERLANDS

Flood

BELARUS

POLAND

Oil spills

GERMANY

BELGIUM

LUXEMBOURG

CZECH REP.

Nuclear accident

FRANCE

SLOVAKIA

UKRAINE

SWITZERLAND

AUSTRIA

HUNGARY

MOLDOVA

Oil spills

Flood

SLOVENIA

ROMANIA

Flood

CROATIA

SPAIN

ANDORRA

BOSNIA & HERZEGOVINA

SERBIA

PORTUGAL

ITALY

MONTENEGRO

BULGARIA

MACEDONIA

ALBANIA

GREECE

Earthquake

MALTA

Earthquake

Environmental damage to land and sea

Area affected by acid rain

▼ Sea dumping sites

Area at risk of desertification

● Worst urban polluters

Most polluted seas

● Major environmental disasters and type

— Most polluted rivers

Natural hazards

Volcanic eruptions occur in southern Italy and Iceland, while earthquakes affect some areas, especially the eastern Mediterranean. Global warming caused by air pollution has begun to change weather patterns.

Unusual weather, such as exceptionally heavy rains and storms, has caused severe floods in some areas, such as France and UK, while extremely high summer temperatures have caused thousands of deaths.

Damaging the environment

The use of smokeless fuels has greatly reduced air pollution in many European cities, but factories, power stations and motor vehicles still pump poisonous gases into the air. These gases are dissolved by water droplets in the air and return to the ground as acid rain. The chemicals kill trees and wildlife in rivers and lakes. Air pollution has also caused global warming and damage to the ozone layer, which protects us from the sun's harmful ultraviolet radiation.

Intensive farming in dry areas, such as southeastern Spain, has turned once fertile land into barren desert. Industrial and agricultural wastes have polluted rivers, while oil spills from tankers have greatly harmed marine life.

Accidents at nuclear power stations have released dangerous nuclear fallout. Europe's worst nuclear accident occurred when explosions and fire damaged a nuclear power plant at Chernobyl, Ukraine, in 1986.

Diseases and deaths

The leading causes of death in western Europe are circulatory diseases (which cause heart attacks and strokes), cancers and car accidents.

Number of deaths each year from cancer per 100,000 people

| 200 | 225 | 250 | 275 | 300 + |

Number of deaths each year from heart disease per 100,000 people

| 100 | 150 | 200 | 250 | 300 + |

Number of deaths each year from road traffic accidents per 100,000 people

| 10 | 15 | 20 | 25 | 30 + |

Eastern European figures not available

Endangered species

During the Ice Age, a lot of animals became extinct as the ice sheets advanced and retreated. However, since the end of the Ice Age, about 10,000 years ago, the land has been transformed into a patchwork of farms and towns. The destruction of habitats has led to some extinctions, while many animals have disappeared from areas that they once inhabited.

Hunting for food and skins, and the slaughter of animals such as bears and wolves to protect domestic animals, have also reduced the ranges of many creatures. Pressures on wildlife remain as the continuing destruction of hedgerows, land reclamation, military exercises and the growth of tourism continue to reduce natural habitats.

Ladies-slipper orchid

Some endangered species in Europe

Mammals
European bison
Horseshoe bat
Ibex
Lynx
Otter

Birds and butterflies
Dalmatian pelican
Golden eagle
Swallowtail butterfly

Marine animals
Common seal
Loggerhead turtle

Trees and plants
Bog pimpernel
Dwarf birch
Irish spurge
Ladies-slipper orchid

ECONOMY

Most European countries are highly developed. They produce large amounts of manufactured goods and farm products, but have to import food and many raw materials. Until the late 1980s, the economies of the Communist countries of eastern Europe were run by their governments but today virtually all of them encourage private ownership and free enterprise.

European Union
To increase trade and to encourage economic growth 27 countries (see right) belong to the European Union, and several others, including Croatia, Macedonia and Turkey, hope to join soon. Some 13 of the nations now share a currency, the euro €.

€ Austria	Latvia
€ Belgium	Lithuania
Bulgaria	€ Luxembourg
Cyprus*	€ Malta
Czech Republic	Poland
Denmark	€ Portugal
Estonia	Romania
€ Finland	Slovakia
€ France	Slovenia
€ Germany	€ Spain
€ Greece	Sweden
Hungary	€ Netherlands
€ Ireland	United Kingdom
€ Italy	

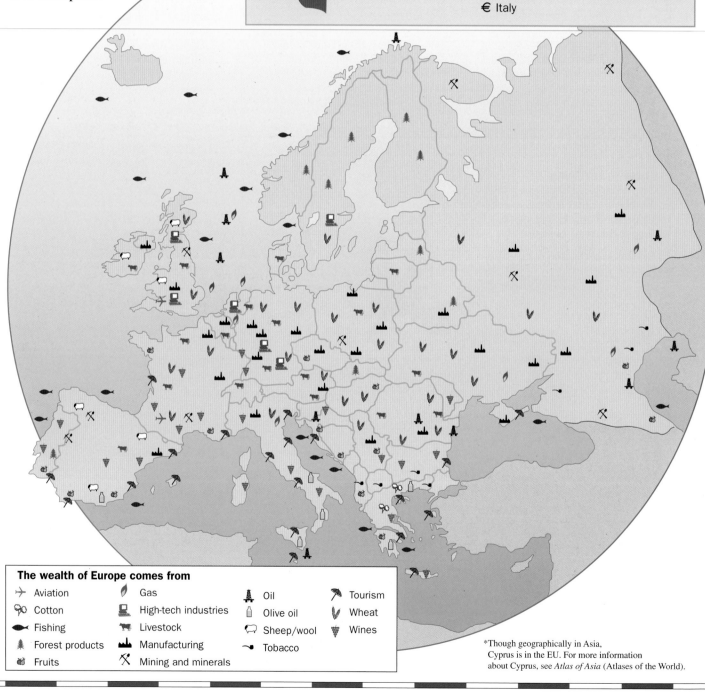

The wealth of Europe comes from

- ✈ Aviation
- ⚺ Cotton
- 🐟 Fishing
- 🌲 Forest products
- 🍎 Fruits
- ◊ Gas
- 💻 High-tech industries
- 🐄 Livestock
- ⛏ Manufacturing
- ⚒ Mining and minerals
- ⛽ Oil
- 🍶 Olive oil
- 🐑 Sheep/wool
- 🚬 Tobacco
- ☂ Tourism
- ⁖ Wheat
- 🍇 Wines

*Though geographically in Asia, Cyprus is in the EU. For more information about Cyprus, see *Atlas of Asia* (Atlases of the World).

Gross domestic product

In order to compare the economies of countries, experts work out the gross domestic product (GDP) of the countries in United States dollars. The GDP is the total value of the goods and services produced by a country in a year. The chart, right, shows that the countries with the highest GDPs in 2005 were Germany, the United Kingdom, France, and Italy. The combined GDP of the 27 members of the European Union is one-tenth larger than that of the United States.

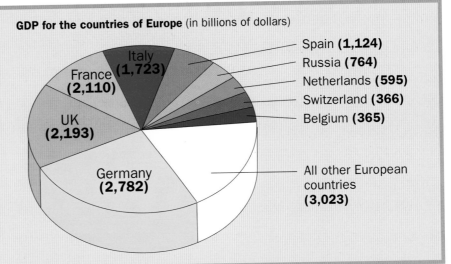

GDP for the countries of Europe (in billions of dollars)

- Italy (1,723)
- France (2,110)
- UK (2,193)
- Germany (2,782)
- Spain (1,124)
- Russia (764)
- Netherlands (595)
- Switzerland (366)
- Belgium (365)
- All other European countries (3,023)

Sources of energy

Coal and hydroelectricity were once the chief sources of power in Europe. Major coal producers are Russia, Ukraine and Poland. Hydroelectricity is important in rainy mountainous countries, such as Norway.

Today, oil and natural gas have become major sources of power, while coal has become less important. Europe's oil producers include Britain and Norway, which share the oilfields in the North Sea, and Russia. Leading natural gas producers include Britain, the Netherlands, Norway and Russia. Major nuclear power-producing countries include France, Germany and Russia. Other sources of energy, including tidal, wind and wave power, are now being developed in Europe.

Per capita GDPs

Per capita means per head or per person. Per capita GDPs are worked out by dividing the GDP by the population. For example, the per capita GDP of the oil-rich country of Norway is US $42,800. By contrast, Albania has a per capita GDP of only $5,300, which places it among the world's poorest countries.

Sources of energy found in Europe

- 🛢 Oil
- 💧 Gas
- ≈ Hydroelectricity
- ⚒ Coal
- ☢ Uranium

POLITICS AND HISTORY

Between the late 1940s and the 1980s, the democratic countries of the West were opposed to the Communist countries in the east. The tension between the groups was called the Cold War. In the 1980s, the collapse of Communism in the Soviet Union and eastern Europe led to the appearance of new countries on the map. In the 1990s, the West helped the former Communist countries to rebuild their economies. The Cold War was over but new kinds of conflict began. In particular, civil wars occurred when rival language and religious groups fought for power in Chechnya, Russia, and in former Yugoslavia.

The Romans dominated Europe with their army. Foot soldiers regularly marched vast distances carrying equipment weighing more than 88lb (40kg).

Great events

After the end of the Ice Age, around 10,000 years ago, the warm climate led to a rapid growth in the human population of Europe. Around 5,000 years ago, civilizations began to develop in the eastern Mediterranean and, between 500 and 300 BCE, the ancient Greek civilization reached its peak. It was succeeded by the Roman Empire, which developed building, law and commerce.

Following the fall of the Roman Empire, there was a period of decline. The early 14th century, however, saw the beginning of a period, known for its brilliant art and a revival of learning, called the Renaissance. Towards the end of this period in the 15th and 16th centuries, Europeans began to spread around the world.

The Industrial Revolution began in Europe in the late 18th century. In the late 19th century, Europeans colonized much of the world. The 20th century saw two major world wars and frequent changes to the map of Europe. The European empires and the Cold War came to an end and the century ended with the hope that cooperation between countries could prevent conflict. However, with the new century have come new terrorist threats.

William the Conqueror defeats the Anglo-Saxons 1066

Vikings begin raiding western Europe 793

Russian Revolution 1917

Mongols invade from the east 1236

Irish Potato Famine 1845

Napoleon defeated at Waterloo 1815

Berlin Wall erected 1961

Spanish Armada defeated 1588

Gutenberg prints first book 1445

Communists take over most of eastern Europe 1948

French Revolution 1789

Reformation begins in Germany 1517

Black Death spreads through Europe from southern ports 1346

Visigoths sack Rome 410 CE ending the thousand-year empire

Greek civilizations begin 3200 BCE

20,000 Evidence of cave dwellers in various sites throughout Europe

6500 Farming in Greece

3200 Early Cycladic civilization in Aegean

1600 Rise of Mycenaean civilization in Greece

1200 Collapse of Mycenaean empire

509 Foundation of Roman Republic

400s Ancient Greece reaches its peak

334 Alexander the Great begins his conquests of eastern Europe, Asia and North Africa

43 Roman invasion of Britain

117 Greatest extent of the Roman Empire

410 Visigoths sack Rome

711 Muslim conquest of Spain

793 Viking raids begin

1066 Norman conquest of England

1236 Mongols from Asia attack eastern Europe

1275 Italian explorer Marco Polo reaches China

1290 Spectacles invented in Italy

1337 Hundred Years War between England and France starts

1348 Black Death spreads from Asia, killing an estimated 20 million people

20,000 BCE	1 CE

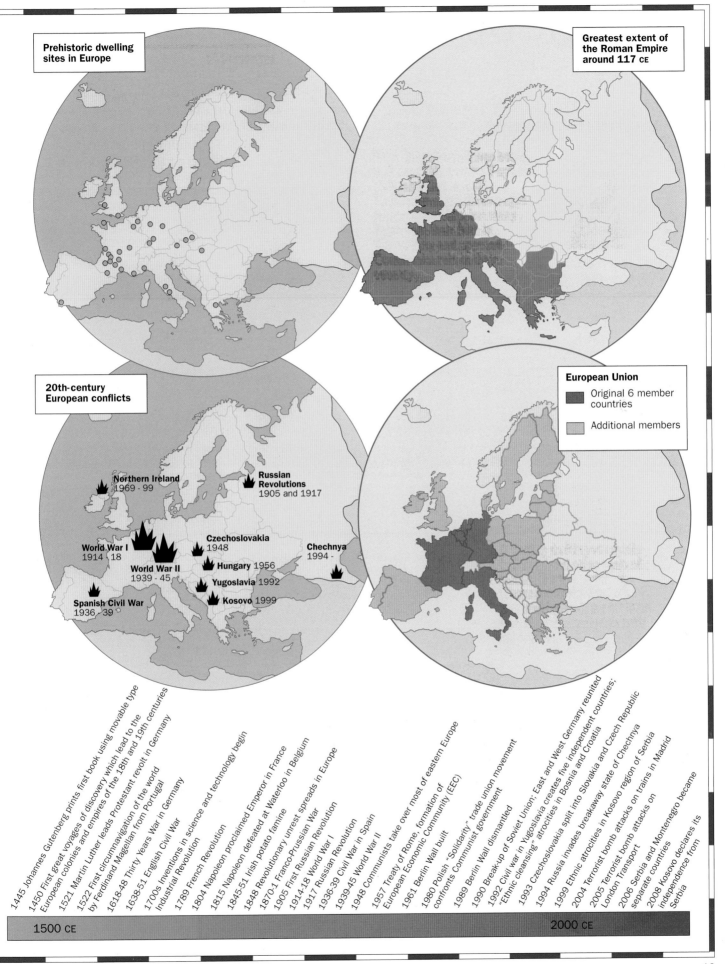

Prehistoric dwelling sites in Europe

Greatest extent of the Roman Empire around 117 CE

European Union

- Original 6 member countries
- Additional members

20th-century European conflicts

Northern Ireland 1969 - 99

Russian Revolutions 1905 and 1917

World War I 1914 - 18

World War II 1939 - 45

Czechoslovakia 1948

Hungary 1956

Chechnya 1994 -

Yugoslavia 1992

Spanish Civil War 1936 - 39

Kosovo 1999

1445 Johannes Gutenberg prints first book using movable type

1450 First great voyages of discovery which lead to the European colonies and empires of the 18th and 19th centuries

1521 Martin Luther leads Protestant revolt in Germany

1522 First circumnavigation of the world by Ferdinand Magellan from Portugal

1618-48 Thirty Years War in Germany

1638-51 English Civil War

1700s Inventions in science and technology begin

Industrial Revolution

1789 French Revolution

1804 Napoleon proclaimed Emperor in France

1815 Napoleon defeated at Waterloo in Belgium

1845-51 Irish potato famine

1848 Revolutionary unrest spreads in Europe

1870-1 Franco-Prussian War

1905 First Russian Revolution

1914-18 World War I

1917 Russian Revolution

1936-39 Civil War in Spain

1939-45 World War II

1948 Communists take over most of eastern Europe

1957 Treaty of Rome, formation of European Economic Community (EEC)

1961 Berlin Wall built

1980 Polish "Solidarity" trade union movement confronts Communist government

1989 Berlin Wall dismantled

1990 Break-up of Soviet Union; East and West Germany reunited

1992 Civil war in Yugoslavia creates five independent countries; "Ethnic cleansing" atrocities in Bosnia and Croatia

1993 Czechoslovakia split into Slovakia and Czech Republic

1994 Russia invades breakaway state of Chechnya

1999 Ethnic atrocities in Kosovo region of Serbia

2004 Terrorist bomb attacks on trains in Madrid

2005 Terrorist bomb attacks on London Transport

2006 Serbia and Montenegro became separate countries

2008 Kosovo declares its independence from Serbia

1500 CE

2000 CE

43

ATLANTIC OCEAN

The Atlantic is the world's second largest ocean after the Pacific. It stretches from the Arctic Ocean around the North Pole to the icy continent of Antarctica around the South Pole. Greenland is the largest of the many islands in the Atlantic Ocean.

Strong currents move through the Atlantic. The warm Gulf Stream starts in the Gulf of Mexico and flows northeast to Europe. It warms coastal areas in northwest Europe. By contrast, the icy Labrador Current flows south from the Arctic and chills the northeastern coasts of North America.

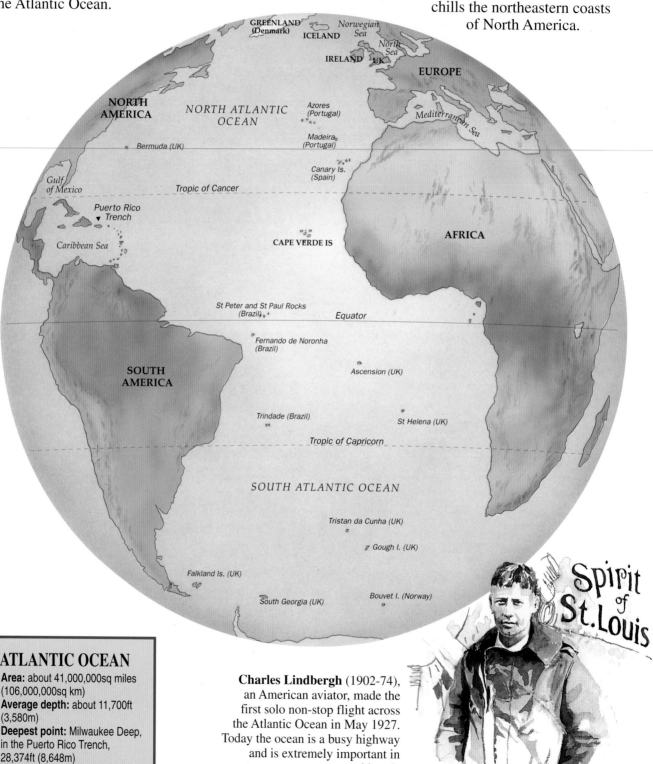

GREENLAND (Denmark)
Norwegian Sea
ICELAND
North Sea
IRELAND UK
EUROPE
NORTH AMERICA
NORTH ATLANTIC OCEAN
Azores (Portugal)
Mediterranean Sea
Bermuda (UK)
Madeira (Portugal)
Gulf of Mexico
Tropic of Cancer
Canary Is. (Spain)
Puerto Rico Trench
AFRICA
CAPE VERDE IS
Caribbean Sea
St Peter and St Paul Rocks (Brazil)
Equator
Fernando de Noronha (Brazil)
SOUTH AMERICA
Ascension (UK)
Trindade (Brazil)
St Helena (UK)
Tropic of Capricorn
SOUTH ATLANTIC OCEAN
Tristan da Cunha (UK)
Gough I. (UK)
Falkland Is. (UK)
Bouvet I. (Norway)
South Georgia (UK)

ATLANTIC OCEAN
Area: about 41,000,000sq miles (106,000,000sq km)
Average depth: about 11,700ft (3,580m)
Deepest point: Milwaukee Deep, in the Puerto Rico Trench, 28,374ft (8,648m)

Charles Lindbergh (1902-74), an American aviator, made the first solo non-stop flight across the Atlantic Ocean in May 1927. Today the ocean is a busy highway and is extremely important in world trade.

Spirit of St. Louis

ARCTIC OCEAN

The Arctic is the smallest of the world's four oceans. It is bordered by North America, Asia and northwestern Europe. It is linked to the Atlantic by the broad Norwegian Sea. The North Pole lies near its center.

Sea ice covers much of the Arctic Ocean, and this stopped early explorers from finding a sea passage that would be a short cut from Europe to the Far East. They searched for a northeast passage north of Asia and a northwest passage north of North America. The first voyage through the Northeast Passage around Asia took place in 1878-9 and the first through the Northwest Passage was first completed in 1906. Neither route was good for trade.

Map labels:

PACIFIC OCEAN
Bering Sea
60°
Arctic Circle
70°
Permanent pack ice
Beaufort Sea
80°
180°
Laptev Sea
120°
ARCTIC OCEAN
North Pole
120°
Severnaya Zemlya (Russia)
Kara Sea
NORTH AMERICA
ASIA
Ellesmere I.
60°
60°
Hudson Bay
Franz Josef Land (Russia)
Novaya Zemlya (Russia)
Baffin Bay
0°
Svalbard (Norway)
Greenland Sea
Barents Sea
GREENLAND (Denmark)
Labrador Sea
Limit of Winter pack ice
Norwegian Sea
ICELAND
ATLANTIC OCEAN
EUROPE

Robert E Peary (1856-1920), a US Navy Commander, was the first explorer to reach the North Pole. He crossed the sea ice with his assistant Matthew Henson and four Inuits, reaching the Pole on April 6, 1909.

ARCTIC OCEAN

Area: about 5,110,000sq miles (13,230,000sq km)
Average depth: about 3,670ft (1,120m)
Deepest point: about 18,044ft (5,550m) north of Svalbard

GLOSSARY

agricultural Having to do with the cultivation of crops and raising of livestock.

amphitheater An open-air structure with seating for large audiences, amphitheaters were venues for theatrical performances and athletic contests.

barge A large boat used to transport materials on rivers and other waterways.

canal An artificially constructed waterway.

castanets A percussion instrument consisting of two small, hollow pieces of wood that are clicked together.

cathedral A large church.

Communism A system of government based on the elimination of private property, a centralized power structure, and the elimination of social class.

denomination A distinct, organized religious faith.

dictatorship A form of government where the citizens don't have democratic rights, and the country is ruled by an authoritarian leader.

dramatist A playwright.

emperor The ruler in command of an empire.

flamenco A kind of dance originated in Andalusia, Spain.

gladiators In ancient Rome, a person who fought, sometimes to the death, in front of an audience.

hedgerow Rows of hedges, bushes, or trees, often planted to separate fields or meadows.

Impressionism Impressionism emphasized personal expression over realism, and dealt with everyday subject matter.

lava Molten rock.

mountaineer A person whole climbs mountains; mountaineers are sometimes referred to as alpinists.

nomadic Wandering from one place to another instead of having a fixed home.

port A place where ships can dock, often for the purpose of loading or unloading cargo.

prosperous Successful or profitable.

textile Cloth or fabric.

tundra Land that is permanently frozen.

FOR MORE INFORMATION

Delegation of the European Commission to the United Nations
222 East 41st Street 20th Floor
New York, NY 10017
(212) 371-3804
Web site: http://www.eu-un.europa.eu/
The United Nations is an international organization that works to mediate disputes between countries, promote security, decide matters of international law, and facilitate economic development. EU member states currently comprise approximately one-third of the UN Security Council.

National Geographic Society
1145 17th Street N.W.
Washington, D.C. 20036-4688
(800) 647-5463
Web site: http://www.nationalgeographic.com/
This non-profit organization promotes science and education, and works to conserve both cultural and natural resources. Established in 1888, it is one of the world's largest educational non-profits.

The Metropolitan Museum of Art
1000 Fifth Avenue.
New York, NY 10028
(212) 535-7710
Web site: http://www.metmuseum.org
The Metropolitan Museum of Art has extensive collections of art from around the world, including European paintings, sculpture, and other cultural treasures. The Museum also has a collection of Ancient Greek and Roman artifacts.

WEB SITES

Due to the changing nature of Internet links, Rosen Publishing has developed an online list of Web sites related to the subject of this book. This site is updated regularly. Please use this link to access the list:

http://www.rosenlinks.com/atl/europe

FOR FURTHER READING

Faiella, Graham. *England: A Primary Source Cultural Guide* (Primary Sources of World Cultures). New York, NY: Rosen Publishing, 2005.

Faiella, Graham. *Spain: A Primary Source Cultural Guide* (Primary Sources of World Cultures). New York, NY: Rosen Publishing, 2004.

Favor, Leslie J. *Italy: A Primary Source Cultural Guide. (Primary Sources of World Cultures)*. New York, NY: Rosen Publishing, 2004.

Horne, William, Zoran Pablovic, and Charles F. Gritzner. *Germany* (Modern World Nations). New York, NY: Chelsea House Publications, 2007.

Kort, Michael. *The Handbook of the New Eastern Europe.* Brookfield, CT: Twenty-First Century Books, 2001.

McDonald, Ferdie, and Claire Marsden, eds. *Europe* (An Eyewitness Travel Guide). New York, NY: Dorling Kindersley Publishing, Inc., 2004.

McGinnis, Maura. *Greece: A Primary Source Cultural Guide. (Primary Sources of World Cultures)*. New York, NY: Rosen Publishing, 2004.

Murrell, Kathleen Berton. *Eyewitness: Russia.* New York, NY: Dorling Kindersley Publishing, Inc., 2000.

Pavlovic, Zoran. *Europe* (Modern World Cultures). New York, NY: Chelsea House Publications, 2006.

Porterfield, Jason. *Sweden: A Primary Source Cultural Guide* (Primary Sources of World Cultures). New York, NY: Rosen Publishing, 2003.

INDEX

ABOUT THE AUTHORS

S. Joshua Comire is a writer living in Queens, New York.

Malcolm Porter is a leading cartographer for children's books. He has contributed to the *Times Atlas* and *Reader's Digest Atlas*, and has provided maps for leading educational and trade publishers. He drew the maps and designed the award-winning books *Atlas of the United States of America* and the *Collins Children's Atlas*.

Keith Lye is a best-selling author of geography titles for children of all ages. He is a distinguished contributor and consultant to major encyclopedias, including *Encyclopedia Britannica and World Book*.